Praise for Charlie LeDuff's *Detroit*

"LeDuff returns, by the book's end, to the bar where his sister was last seen, only to find it unrecognizable. A black man outside explains the changes. 'They trying to put something nice up' in this hellhole, he says, speaking of the bar specifically, though his words spread across the city and pay tribute, in equal measure, to its dreamers, its pessimists and to those, resigned and wrung out, who love it despite all. 'Can't say it's working. But what you gonna do? You ain't gonna be reincarnated, so you got to do the best you can with the moment you got. Do the best you can and try to be good.' LeDuff has done his best, and his book is better than good." —Paul Clemens, *The New York Times Book Review*

"One cannot read Mr. LeDuff's amalgam of memoir and reportage and not be shaken by the cold eye he casts on hard truths. . . . A little gonzo, a little gumshoe, some gawker, some Good Samaritan—it is hard to ignore reporting like Mr. LeDuff's." —*The Wall Street Journal*

"Pulitzer Prize–winning journalist LeDuff (*Work and Other Sins*) delivers an edgy portrait of the decline, destruction, and possible redemption of his hometown. . . . LeDuff writes with honesty and compassion about a city that's destroying itself—and breaking his heart." —*Publishers Weekly* (starred review)

"This is our pick for a sleeper nonfiction hit next year. Charlie LeDuff is a remarkable journalist, and this book is filled with incredible writing as he witnesses his home city crumble through neglect and corruption." —*The Huffington Post*

"What to do when you're a reporter and your native city is rotting away? If you're LeDuff, you leave *The New York Times* and head into the wreckage to ride with firemen, hang with the corrupt pols, and retrace your own family's sad steps through drugs. Others have written well about the city, but none with the visceral anger, the hair-tearing frustration, and the hungry humanity of LeDuff."   —*Newsweek*

"You wouldn't think a book about the stinking decay of the American dream could be this engaging, this irreverent, this laugh-out-loud funny. But not everyone can write like Charlie LeDuff. I'm tempted to say he's the writer for our desperate times the way Steinbeck and Orwell were for other people's desperate times, except he's such an original he's like no one but himself."

—Alexandra Fuller, author of *Cocktail Hour Under the
Tree of Forgetfulness* and *Don't Let's Go to the Dogs Tonight*

"Charlie LeDuff is a drunkard, a blowhard, a Fox News reporter—and a brilliant writer. *Detroit* is full of righteous anger and heartbreaking details. It's also funny as hell. Hunter S. Thompson would've loved every page of this book."

—Eric Schlosser, author of *Command and Control* and *Fast Food Nation*

"In *Detroit: An American Autopsy*, Charlie LeDuff brings alive the reality of our beloved city. The city where I was shot at eight times during my twenty-six-year police career. Yet, Detroit has survived in spite of corruption, political ineptness, poor education, and decades of unemployment. *Detroit: An American Autopsy* is a must-read for all of America."

—Detroit Police Chief Ike McKinnon (retired);
associate professor of education, University of Detroit Mercy

PENGUIN BOOKS

DETROIT

Charlie LeDuff was a staff writer at *The New York Times* and a reporter at the *Detroit News* and is now a television journalist for Detroit's Fox 2 News. He contributed to a Pulitzer Prize–winning *New York Times* series and has received a Meyer Berger Award for distinguished writing about New York City. He is the author of *US Guys* and *Work and Other Sins*. LeDuff lives with his wife and daughter on the edge of the Detroit city limits.

DETROIT

AN AMERICAN AUTOPSY

CHARLIE LEDUFF

PENGUIN BOOKS

PENGUIN BOOKS
Published by the Penguin Group
Penguin Group (USA) LLC
375 Hudson Street
New York, New York 10014

USA | Canada | UK | Ireland | Australia | New Zealand | India | South Africa | China
penguin.com
A Penguin Random House Company

First published in the United States of America by The Penguin Press,
a member of Penguin Group (USA) Inc., 2013
This edition with a revised epilogue published in Penguin Books 2014

"Evidence Detroit," photographs by Danny Wilcox Frazier
Quote on page ix from *Divided Soul: The Life of Marvin Gaye* by David Ritz (Da Capo Press, 2003)

THE LIBRARY OF CONGRESS HAS CATALOGED THE HARDCOVER EDITION AS FOLLOWS:
LeDuff, Charlie.
Detroit : an American autopsy / Charlie LeDuff.
p. cm.
ISBN 978-1-59420-534-7 (hc.)
ISBN 978-0-14-312446-7 (pbk.)
1. Detroit (Mich.)—Economic conditions. 2. Detroit (Mich.)—Social conditions. 3. Detroit (Mich.)—
Politics and government. 4. LeDuff, Charlie. 5. Journalists—Michigan—Detroit—Biography. I. Title.
HC108.D6L44 2013
977.4'34044—dc23
2012030924

Printed in the United States of America
5 7 9 10 8 6

Book Design by Claire Naylon Vaccaro

For Amy and Claudette

Detroit turned out to be heaven,

but it also turned out to be hell.

—Marvin Gaye

CONTENTS

ACKNOWLEDGMENTS

Corn does not grow alone. And books do not write themselves. I'd like to give thanks to the people of Detroit, Michigan, U.S.A.—especially those who shared their stories here. You are a proud nation.

My mother, Evangeline, who taught me my first words, told me our family stories and showed me how to write my name. You are the rock.

My brothers Jim, Frank and Bill. Without you, I would have grown up a weakling.

My wife, Amy, who endures the journey—both high and low. Thanks for holding my hand, baby.

Some material in this book appeared in different form in both the *Detroit News* and *Mother Jones* magazine. My gratitude to Jon Wolman, publisher and editor of the *News*, as well as Gary Miles and Walter Middlebrook, for bringing me home.

My colleagues at the *News*—especially Max Ortiz and Elizabeth Conley for their photographic eyes and friendship on all those cold nights. Bob Houlihan, Paul Egan, Joel Kurth, George Hunter, Doug Guthrie and Laura Berman—for their generosity and outlook.

Clara Jeffery at *Mother Jones*: thank you for helping me see it.

Scott Burgess wrote for me a long description of the goings-on at the Los Angeles Auto Show, much of which is quoted here. My appreciation for the assist and the insight.

Todd Schindler provided a keen eye and solid shoulder when things got tough. Bob Paris came up with the title for the book.

Sloan Harris and Ann Godoff. Without their strong arms, this boat would have sunk.

Danny Frazier. Remember what the sign says: Stay Inn.

Thanks to the Mongo brothers: Adolph, Larry and Skip. Your pool runs deep.

The men and women of the Detroit Police Department, especially Mike Carlisle, Tony Wright and Mike Martel, and all those in blue whose names I cannot print. You know why. Respect.

The men and women of the Detroit Fire Department: Mike Nevin, Wisam Zeineh and the crazy sons of bitches who do the job because the job's got to be done.

Every teacher who helps and every honest politician who serves.

Claudette: remember where you come from, girl. Sometime in her life a bird needs to circle home.

DETROIT

PROLOGUE

I REACHED DOWN the pant cuff with the eraser end of my pencil and poked it. Frozen solid. But definitely human.

"Goddamn."

I took a deep breath through my cigarette. I didn't want to use my nose. It was late January, the air scorching cold. The snow was falling sideways as it usually did in Detroit this time of year. The dead man was encased in at least four feet of ice at the bottom of a defunct elevator shaft in an abandoned building. But still, there was no telling what the stink might be like.

I couldn't make out his face. The only things protruding above the ice were the feet, dressed in some white sweat socks and a pair of black gym shoes. I could see the hem of his jacket below the surface. The rest of him tapered off into the void.

In most cities, a death scene like this would be considered re-markable, mind-blowing, horrifying. But not here. Something had happened in Detroit while I was away.

. . .

I had left the city two decades earlier to try to make a life for myself that didn't involve a slow death working in a chemical factory or a liquor store. Any place but those places.

But where? I wandered for years, working my way across Asia, Europe, the Arctic edge working as a cannery hand, a carpenter, a drifter. And then I settled into the most natural thing for a man with no real talents.

Journalism.

It required no expertise, no family connections and no social graces. Furthermore, it seemed to be the only job that paid you to travel, excluding a door-to-door Bible salesman. Nearly thirty years old, I went back to school to study the inverted pyramid of writing. I landed my first newspaper job with the *Alaska Fisherman's Journal,* where I wrote dispatches in longhand on legal pads and mailed them back to headquarters in Seattle.

So I went out into the Last Frontier with my notepad and a tent and wrote what I saw: stuff about struggling fishermen, a mountain woman who drank too much and dried her panties on a line stretched across the bow of her boat, Mexican laborers forced to live in the swamps, a prince who lived under a bridge, a gay piano man on a fancy cruise liner. People managing somehow. My kind of people. The job suited me.

Working off that, I tried to land a real job but couldn't find one. The *Detroit Free Press* didn't want me. Not the *San Francisco Chronicle.* Not the *Oakland Tribune.* I was thinking about returning to the Alaskan fishing boats until a little Podunk paper called me with an offer of a summer internship—the *New York Times.*

Luck counts too.

I ended up working at the Gray Lady for a decade, sketching the lives of hustlers and working stiffs and firemen at Ground Zero. It was a good run. But wanderlust is like a pretty girl—you wake up one morning, find she's grown old and decide that either you're going to commit your life or you're going to walk away. I walked away, and as it happens in life, I circled home, taking a job with the *Detroit News*. My colleagues in New York laughed. The paper was on death watch. And so was the city.

It is important to note that, growing up in Detroit and its suburbs, I can honestly say it was never that good in the first place. People of older generations like to tell me about the swell old days of soda fountains and shopping stores and lazy Saturday night drives. But the fact is Detroit was dying forty years ago when the Japanese began to figure out how to make a better car. The whole country knew the city and the region was on the skids, and the whole country laughed at us. A bunch of lazy, uneducated blue-collar incompetents. The Rust Belt. The Rust Bowl. Forget about it. Florida was calling.

No one cared much about Detroit until the Dow collapsed in 2008, the economy melted down and the chief executives of the Big Three went to Washington, D.C., to grovel. Suddenly the eyes of the nation turned back upon this postindustrial sarcophagus, where crime and corruption and mismanagement and mayhem played themselves out in the corridors of power and on the powerless streets. Detroit became epic, historic, symbolic, hip even. I began to get calls from reporters around the world wondering what the city was like, what was happening here. They wondered if the Rust Belt cancer had metastasized and was creeping toward Los Angeles and London and Barcelona. Was Detroit an outlier or an epicenter? Was Detroit a symbol of the greater decay? Is the Motor City the future of

America? Are we living through a cycle or an epoch? Suddenly they weren't laughing out there anymore.

Journalists parachuted into town. The subjects in my *Detroit News* stories started appearing in *Rolling Stone* and the *Wall Street Journal*, on NPR and PBS and CNN, but under someone else's byline. The reporters rarely, if ever, offered nuanced appraisals of the city and its place in the American landscape. They simply took a tour of the ruins, ripped off the local headlines, pronounced it awful here and left.

And it is awful here, there is no other way to say it. But I believe that Detroit is America's city. It was the vanguard of our way up, just as it is the vanguard of our way down. And one hopes the vanguard of our way up again. Detroit is Pax Americana. The birthplace of mass production, the automobile, the cement road, the refrigerator, frozen peas, high-paid blue-collar jobs, home ownership and credit on a mass scale. America's way of life was built here.

It's where installment purchasing on a large scale was invented in 1919 by General Motors to sell their cars. It was called the Arsenal of Democracy in the 1940s, the place where the war machines were made to stop the march of fascism.

So important was the Detroit way of doing things that its automobile executives in the fifties and sixties went to Washington and imprinted the military with their management style and structure. Robert McNamara was the father of the Ford Falcon and the architect of the Vietnam War. Charlie Wilson was the president of General Motors and Eisenhower's man at the Pentagon, who famously said he thought that "what was good for our country was good for General Motors, and vice versa."

If what Wilson said is true, then so too must be its opposite.

Today, the boomtown is bust. It is an eerie and angry place of deserted factories and homes and forgotten people. Detroit, which once led the nation in home ownership, is now a foreclosure capital. Its downtown is a museum of ghost skyscrapers. Trees and switchgrass and wild animals have come back to reclaim their rightful places. Coyotes are here. The pigeons have left in droves. A city the size of San Francisco and Manhattan could neatly fit into Detroit's vacant lots, I am told.

Once the nation's richest big city, Detroit is now its poorest. It is the country's illiteracy and dropout capital, where children must leave their books at school and bring toilet paper from home. It is the unemployment capital, where half the adult population does not work at a consistent job. There are firemen with no boots, cops with no cars, teachers with no pencils, city council members with telephones tapped by the FBI, and too many grandmothers with no tears left to give.

But Detroit can no longer be ignored, because what happened here is happening out there. Neighborhoods from Phoenix to Los Angeles to Miami are blighted with empty houses and people with idle hands. Americans are swimming in debt, and the prospects of servicing the debt grow slimmer by the day as good-paying jobs continue to evaporate or relocate to foreign lands. Economists talk about the inevitable turnaround. But standing here in Michigan, it seems to me that the fundamentals are no longer there to make the good life.

Go ahead and laugh at Detroit. Because you are laughing at yourself.

In cities and towns across the country, whole factories are auctioned off. Men with trucks haul away tool-and-die machines, aluminum siding, hoists, drinking fountains. It is the ripping out of the country's mechanical heart right before our eyes.

A newly hired autoworker will earn $14 an hour. This, adjusted for inflation, is three cents *less* than what Henry Ford was paying in 1914 when he announced the $5 day. And, of course, Ford isn't hiring.

Come to Detroit. Drive the empty, shattered boulevards, and the decrepitude of the place all rolls out in a numb, continuous fact. After enough hours staring into it, it starts to appear normal. Average. Everyday.

And then you come across something like a man frozen in ice and the skeleton of the anatomy of the place reveals itself to you.

The neck bone is connected to the billionaire who owns the crumbling building where the man died. The rib bones are connected to the countless minions shuffling through the frostbitten streets burning fires in empty warehouses to stay warm—and get high. The hip bone is connected to a demoralized police force who couldn't give a shit about digging a dead mope out of an elevator shaft. The thigh bone is connected to the white suburbanites who turn their heads away from the calamity of Detroit, carrying on as though the human suffering were somebody else's problem. And the foot bones—well, they're sticking out of a block of dirty frozen water, belonging to an unknown man nobody seemed to give a rip about.

We are not alone on this account. Across the country, the dead go unclaimed in the municipal morgues because people are too poor to bury their loved ones: Los Angeles, New York, Chicago. It's the same. Grandpa is on layaway while his family tries to scratch together a box and a plot.

This is not a book about geopolitics or macroeconomics or global finance. And it is not a feel-good story with a happy ending. It is a book of reportage. A memoir of a reporter returning home— only he cannot find the home he once knew. This is a book about living people getting on with the business of surviving in a place that has little use for anyone anymore except those left here. It is about waking up one morning and being told you are obsolete and not wanting to believe it but knowing it's true. It is a book about a rough town and a tough people during arguably some of the most historic and cataclysmic years in the American experience. It is a book about family and cops and criminals and factory workers. It is about corrupt politicians and a collapsing newspaper. It is about angry people fighting and crying and snatching hold of one another trying to stay alive.

It is about the future of America and our desperate efforts to save ourselves from it.

At the end of the day, the Detroiter may be the most important American there is because no one knows better than he that we're all standing at the edge of the shaft.

ONE
FIRE

GRA-*SHIT*

I PULLED INTO the station, the needle riding on "E."

It was a mistake. In Detroit, if possible, you don't get your gas on the east side, not even at high noon. Because the east side of Motown is Dodge City—semilawless and crazy. Many times citizens don't bother phoning the cops. And as if to return the favor, many times cops don't bother to come.

It was gray and moist on Gratiot Avenue—pronounced Gra-*shit*—a main artery running from the center of the city into the eastern suburbs and up farther still into the countryside. Six lanes wide and not a soul. Not a car. Not a bus. Just steam clouds billowing from the sewer caps. I went inside the gas station, paid $10 to the Arab behind the bulletproof glass and went outside to pump my gas.

A man crept up from the grayness. I didn't make him until he was standing at my front bumper. Another mistake. You always keep your back to the gas pump, eyes on the horizons.

The dude's eyes were dead, cold, flat-black like a skillet's underside. His hair was nappy. He was thin like a stray and his coat was dirty.

"My man," he said too cheerfully. "You got a smoke?"

I pulled a pack from my jacket pocket and gave him one, hoping he'd beat it.

He put the cigarette behind his ear, lingering, offering no thanks.

"You're welcome," I said, hoping to put a period on the meeting and that he'd just walk away.

Another mistake. Charity can be dangerous. He'd made a mark.

"My man," he said, in a tone not so friendly this time. "Got some spare change?"

"Spare change?" I said. "This is America, bro. There is no such thing anymore as spare change."

"HE SAID MONEY MOTHERFUCKER!"

The command came from the rear bumper, where a second man had stalked up without me noticing. He was bigger, darker, more wild-eyed than the first. He had two gold-framed incisors. Cheap work, I thought, like the Mexicans get.

"I spent my last ten on gas, dog," I said, trying to recuperate some of the shattered cool. "Lemme check in there." I pointed toward the glove box.

I bent into the car, reaching for the glove box latch. There was a 9 mm inside. Not mine. It belonged to a reporter who had forgotten to store it in his desk on his way to a press conference. He had asked me in the parking lot to hold on to it and I laughed about a journalist carrying a concealed weapon. Correspondents don't do that even in war zones, I told him.

"Well, how many of those war reporters do you know who've been to Detroit?" he asked me.

I couldn't name him one.

Now here I was on the grubby east side—a war zone in its own right. A place of Used-to-Haves. And a Used-to-Have is an infinitely more dangerous type of man than the habitual Have-Not. This type of man is waging his own war. Not against the power but against his own, a fight much easier to find at the gas pump than on Wall Street.

I emerged from the car and pointed the barrel square toward the man's face.

I said nothing. No Dirty Harry line. No crime novel metaphor. I didn't even know where the safety was or if there was a safety or ammunition in it. I pissed myself a little.

"Okay now," Goldie-mouth said, backing his way into the mist. The other ran like a jackrabbit. The Arab behind the Plexiglas came to the front door after they were long gone.

"You all right, bro?" he shouted.

"Yeah," I said.

"I don't mean to sound funny, bro," he said, giving my vest and tie the once-over. "But what's a white boy doing getting gas on Gra-*shit*?"

Newsroom

THE MOVERS WERE packing my house in Los Angeles when the news broke from Detroit. Someone had slipped the *Free Press* a cache of text messages showing that the city's mayor, Kwame Kilpatrick, was a criminal and a pimp.

Kilpatrick had denied in a court of law that he had fired the police department's chief of internal affairs because he was getting too close to an alleged sex party at the mayor's mansion—where rumor had it that a stripper named "Strawberry" was beaten silly with a high heel by the mayor's wife.

Strawberry—real name Tamara Greene—later turned up murdered.

Kilpatrick had also denied in court that he had had an adulterous affair with his chief of staff, an old girlfriend from high school. The text messages, however, confirmed that not only was Kilpatrick carrying on with his chief of staff, he was a crook who was looting the city and a letch who bagged more tail than a deer hunter.

Worse still, the texts revealed that Kilpatrick secretly spent $10 million of the people of Detroit's money to make the internal affairs whistleblower go away.

It was a huge scoop that cemented the *News'* lowly, stepbrother standing to the rival *Free Press*. My stomach dropped. I called the paper's deputy managing editor back in Detroit.

"What the hell happened?" I asked.

"I don't know," he said.

"This is bad."

"It isn't good," he said. "But don't worry about it. We chased it and got something up on the Web."

Don't worry about it? Chased it? Got something up on the Web? What the hell had I done?

My career with the *New York Times* died in the mountains of Vermont. I was on a story and did not receive the prior evening's voice mail until early in the morning when I arrived at the Burlington airport.

The message was hysterical.

"Charlie. Amy's in the hospital. She went into early labor. Where are you?"

I didn't want to be that guy, the self-absorbed man who was never around for his children. I didn't want to be my father or my first stepfather. It didn't matter that I was working on assignment for the paper. A workaholic is the same as an alcoholic when you get down to it.

"I'm sorry, sir, but your flight is for *next* Sunday," the counter attendant said. "There is nothing available today."

I vomited.

A Latino came and cleaned up my mess. The frantic attendant typed through the computer and found an emergency seat for me out of Burlington to Los Angeles with a change in Chicago.

My baby girl came in at four pounds and I got there to cut the umbilical cord. She was small but strong, and after the second night we were able to go home.

As my girls took a nap, I shaved my whiskers and washed away the smell of puke and cigarettes. Then I filed my story about the Green Party candidate for governor of Vermont, who pranced around town dressed as Ethan Allen, the eighteenth-century American patriot. His platform was a unique one, I thought. It tapped into a smoldering populist anger: screw the federal government and the state police and the big banks. Vermont should secede from the United States.

Looking back on it now, in light of the Tea Party phenomenon, General Allen was ahead of his time. The guy made me laugh anyway, posing for my video camera with a horse he couldn't ride, getting dragged through the mud and dung of the paddock. I smiled at the thought of him and hit "send."

The next day I got an e-mail response from my editor in Manhattan.

"This guy is a loser," she wrote. "He doesn't say anything. What happened to the professor you were going to write about? We have to talk."

I was now writing and producing a video column called "American Album." The conceit was simple. Go across the country and find regular Americans and make stories and videos about them using their language and point of view and post it on the Internet. The work was popular with readers but not with the editor. And at the *Times*, it is not the reader who matters so much.

The editor called the farmers and hunters and drive-through attendants and factory workers I wrote about losers. Say the word slowly enough and it sounds like you're spitting.

Losers.

Losers. That was 80 percent of the country, and the new globalized economic structure was cranking out more. I could see it in my travels. I could see it when I went home to Detroit for the holidays. Hell, I could see it in the box stores on Sunset Boulevard and the FOR SALE signs in the Los Angeles foothills. Walmart was crowded and factories were empty. This was 2007 and people were scared. It felt like the warm mundane bliss of house-rich America was slowly unraveling. I could see it like an oncoming storm. In New York City you could see it too if you bothered to venture above Ninety-sixth Street. We were crumbling under the weight of our own abundance.

I grew bored with the intellectual mud wrestling and the oblique putdowns. Losers. I quit the *Times*.

I also grew bored with Los Angeles. I no longer belonged since I was no longer a writer. I had become a stay-at-home dad, isolated in my Hollywood bungalow with a howling baby and dirty diapers.

I realized how cut off and disconnected we were. We had to cross two major boulevards just to find a park. We had no family out there. We barely knew the neighbors.

Los Angeles may have the weather, but we were isolated in the rush-hour traffic that seemed to run from dawn till dawn. I had no desire to raise an only child in the City of Angels. I was convinced she'd grow into a self-centered little devil, walking the sidewalks of Melrose Avenue at too early an age, wearing too much blue mascara and a halter top, showing off her undeveloped breasts.

I wrote about it for a glamour magazine. Big Shot Quits the Big Time, Sits Home with a Baby and Feels Sorry for Himself.

The governor won't call anymore. Neither will the old colleagues. There will be no more Hollywood parties. No expense account. No action. It will be just you and the kid. And the kid will have no idea how good you were. And worse, in the mania of your empty house . . . when the afternoon sun is bright and debilitating and that old deadline time, that hour of adrenaline, is upon you, right about then you will wonder whether you were really any good at all. You will find yourself staring into a dirty diaper as though it were tea leaves, trying to augur some story about the failings of the last immigration bill.

None of the old colleagues did call. But a letter arrived at my door in mid-November, a few weeks after the story ran. It was from Governor Schwarzenegger, whom I'd met on the campaign trail, the postage paid by the taxpayers of the Golden State, who were drowning in a sea of red ink.

He had read the lines for what they were: a rambling confession of self-doubt. And if there was one thing Schwarzenegger did not possess, it was self-doubt.

"I know you got all kinds of advice from friends, from Oprah-like wisdom to complete ignorance, so I don't have anything to add to that," he wrote. "Just know that what you're doing will be more fulfilling than any of your wild adventures—in fact, it might be your wildest yet—and any father would die to have the life you have."

He told me in essence to follow my gut, do what I thought was right for myself and my family and go snatch life by the throat.

He closed with this: "If you ever start to feel unimportant, you're wrong. But you can always relive the glory days, tell people about your buddy who can lift you up with a finger and runs the biggest state in the world, or give me a call. I'd love to hear about your new assignment."

Far be it from me to take life advice from a guy who starred in *Kindergarten Cop*, but Schwarzenegger only confirmed what I had already known. It was time to go home.

Part of it was for my daughter. Back in Detroit, there were grandparents, aunts and uncles and cousins. There was a culture. A family.

Part of it was for me. I felt like wood sitting there at four o'clock in the Los Angeles afternoon, with nothing to do and no one to talk with but the Armenian next door who could barely speak English.

In the meantime, the wheels were starting to fall off the American party bus, even in Los Angeles. When I first arrived, the average house would sell in less than a week. Now it was six months if it was a day.

Circling back to Detroit was instinct, like a salmon needing to swim upstream because he is genetically encoded to do so. Detroit might be the epicenter, a funhouse mirror and future projection of America. An incredibly depressed city in its death swoon.

But it also could be a Candy Land from a reporter's perspective. Decay. Mile after mile of rotten buildings, murder, leftover people. One fucking depressing, dysfunctional big glowing ball of color. One unbelievable story after another.

Why not admit it? I am a reporter. A leech. A merchant of misery. Bad things are good for us reporters. We are body collectors of sorts. To tell the truth, it is amusing to be a correspondent, the guy who drops in with his parachute, proclaims to know everything, makes outrageous proclamations, types it up, gets drunk in the hotel lounge, folds up his parachute, packs up his hangover and heads to the next spot of human misery.

I'd been everywhere in my decade for the *Times*, looking for the weird. I'm in the weird business. In Detroit, I guessed, I wouldn't have to go looking hard for weird. Weird would find me. I'd treat it like the parachute correspondent, get my nails dirty for a year or two, let my mother hug the kid and then move on.

In the weeks and months that followed, I pitched all the big media outlets from my home in L.A. How about Detroit, I asked? Detroit is a good story. *The story.* A train wreck.

No thanks, they told me. Detroit was nothing. Besides, the newspaper and magazine businesses were crumbling and the last thing any executive editor was willing to do was spend the money to open a boutique bureau in Dead City.

Finally, I swallowed my big-shot pride and called the *Detroit News*. A paper so broke, it didn't even put out a Sunday edition anymore. Surprisingly, they had an opening. Come do what you do, they told me. Chronicle the decline of the Great Industrial American City.

I accepted the offer. And I made myself a promise. I'd build a castle of words so high on the banks of the Detroit River that they couldn't help but see it from Times Square.

The day I began work at the *News* in March 2008, half the lights in the newsroom were off. I was told half jokingly that it was an effort to save on the electricity bill. I was shown to my desk, where I was greeted by a broken chair, a broken phone and a large stain on the carpet that reminded me of one of those old chalk outlines at a homicide scene. The computer would not boot up. The four cubicles that surrounded mine were empty, the papers and pens from the last occupants still there. Like the *Times'* newsroom, the place was as quiet as a meat locker, but there was no doubt, this place was in a lower ring of hell.

A loop of the thirty-eight-year-old Kilpatrick—who fancied himself something of a player and preferred white homburgs and diamond earrings—was playing over and over on a row of television sets embedded in the wall above the editors' desks. Speculation was rampant that the prosecutor was going to file charges against the mayor any day now for his alleged perjury, among other things.

The television images of Kilpatrick were dark and murky since the sets were failing from continual use and the company was too broke to replace them. The screens were doing to the mayor what *Time* magazine editors did to O. J. Simpson—making him appear darker and more sinister.

I got the feeling then that those TVs were bellwethers, canaries in a coal mine. Once they went black, the final grains of sand in the 135-year-old *Detroit News* would run out.

The television reports intimated that the mayor ordered the killing of the stripper Strawberry because of what she knew about the party and the powerful men who attended.

And Kilpatrick was crumbling under the pressure. During his State of the City speech the evening before, he had taken a bizarre detour from his script, ripping the president of the city council as a "step 'n' fetchit" and liberally dropping the "N" bomb, saying he was getting threats and hate mail—ostensibly from the crackers out in the suburbs.

In the best of times, the out-of-town news coverage of Detroit is never very good. There was once a story about a murderer who had to go to Toledo to turn himself in because the Detroit cops wouldn't pay attention to him. *Forbes* had recently named the Motor City the most miserable town in America. But this guy Kilpatrick was taking it to a whole new level. Strippers? Murders? It was a reporter's dream. Suddenly I didn't mind the busted chair so much.

Did the mayor really kill a call girl? I asked the reporters around me. I was told the rumor was five years old but had taken on new life as the central plot in the text-message scandal of the incredible shrinking mayor.

I needed a home run. A calling card. A sizzler that announced: CHARLIE IS HERE.

A murdered stripper on an ordered hit from city hall would fit the bill!

I called a detective I knew.

THIS AIN'T HOLLYWOOD

MIKE CARLISLE WAS considered one of the finest homicide detectives in a place perpetually battling for the title of Murder Capital USA.

He solved well over half his cases in a city with more than eleven thousand unsolved homicides dating back to 1960. Carlisle prided himself on earning his money, even though generally nobody gives a shit about dead prostitutes and dope dealers.

I'd met him a few years earlier while I was in Detroit on assignment for the *Times*. He appealed to me right away: his perpetual cigarette and his cotton-field vocabulary, his workingman suits and the white mustache. He looked and thought like a murder dick should, it seemed to me. He kept an odd collection of photographs in his top desk drawer. A mix of wedding pictures, vacation shots and crime-scene snaps of naked hookers laid out starfish style.

Carlisle answered the phone.

"How's it going, Mike?" I said.

"How's it going? This department is a fucked-up shit hole, Charlie. Nine months to retirement and I'm outta here."

"Nothing's changed, huh?"

"Not a goddamned thing."

I asked if he knew anything about this Strawberry Greene case.

"Yeah, I know something about it," he said. "They've reopened her investigation since numb-nuts got caught texting with his cock, and I'm the asshole whose desk it landed on. It's three binders thick."

"You got that case? No shit?"

"No shit. What are you doing back in town?"

I explained it. He laughed. "That's the dumbest decision I've heard in quite some while. Welcome home, I guess."

"Don't rub it in," I said, staring at the coffee stain at my feet.

I asked if I could see the files.

He brought them the next morning to a diner on Woodward, the main thoroughfare from the city out to the suburbs. We met just north of the city limits, where I had recently bought a house. The fact was, I couldn't afford to live in the ghetto. I loved Detroit, but now that I had a daughter, I wasn't going to live there. Not with the corruption and high taxes and lack of ambulances. So I cast my lot about a mile outside the city proper.

Carlisle sat in a corner, near the front, in a cloud of smoke. You could still smoke in the restaurants in Michigan. He was drinking black coffee.

We made small talk and then ordered. He got oatmeal. Fucking oatmeal and cigarettes. How precious.

"This case ain't shit," Carlisle whispered, looking at the whelp of a waiter who was trying to steal in on the conversation. "It's a dope beef gone wrong. A working girl caught in the middle."

"Is that right?"

"Yeah, but on the other hand, you're fucking with some bad people here. From the mayor on down. This whole town is just a worm-infested shit pile, Charlie. I mean, there are good people, but they get lost in the incompetence. It's a dead city. And anybody says any different doesn't know what the fuck he's talking about."

He was smoking like wet wool. "You know, I took this job because I thought I could make a difference. Because I really thought I could be some help." He pushed the files toward me. "Here, you've got forty minutes."

I began scribbling in my notebook.

He was silent for a few minutes before launching into a monologue about his grandson's new Easter suit. I played along for as long as I could, absently nodding my head while trying to decipher the police reports.

"Mike," I finally said, looking up from the case file. "I've got forty fucking minutes here. Please."

Carlisle stuffed a cigarette in it.

The murder of Tamara "Strawberry" Greene had become the stuff of Detroit legend, a whodunit of sex and politics and power. The most incredible plot was a simple one: she is said to have danced at a party at the mayor's mansion and was executed on the orders of Kilpatrick because she knew the names and proclivities of the powerful attendees.

She died in a hail of bullets in a drive-by shooting nearly a year later, the story went: slumped over her steering wheel, her eye-glasses broken, the car still in drive, creeping down the street. Her boyfriend—a dope dealer—survived.

It was just another murder in a city with too many of them, until the original homicide detective filed a lawsuit after being removed from the case. He claimed that it was Detroit police officers who killed her at the behest of city hall.

But nothing in the case files suggested anything like that. She was not shot eighteen times in a drive-by as that detective claimed; she was struck three times.

The medical examiner's report revealed she died with two black eyes—giving credence to statements given by another stripper that Strawberry was beaten at a party two weeks before her death—the object of affection between two feuding dope dealers.

Then there was the recollection of a drug kingpin doing time in federal prison. Being a kingpin, all dope-related hits on the city's east side had to be cleared through him. So a few weeks after Strawberry's murder, one of the dope dealers came to explain that he was actually trying to shoot her boyfriend.

"Old girl just got in the way," the dope dealer told the kingpin, according to the reports.

Looking at the case file was like looking at the high school yearbook of my sister, Nicole. A beautiful woman tied up in an ugly life. Strawberry oozed sex. And she used it. She teased dangerous men, manipulated them and stole from them. And in the end she paid with her life. A Good Time Girl Who Met a Bad End in the Streets of Detroit.

Strawberry.

Nicole.

A simple book. Made in Detroit.

"How many girls like this die in the city?" I said, looking up at Carlisle.

"Too many," he said, through a cloud of smoke.

"My sister died like this," I told him. "In Detroit."

"Oh, man. I'm sorry."

"She wasn't garbage, you know?"

"She was somebody's daughter," he said sympathetically.

"Yeah, nobody cared at all. Except one cop. A guy named Snarski. I'll never forget his name. Snarski. He understood that everybody's somebody to someone. He got the guy."

"I'll never forget his name either," Carlisle said. "He's the guy who trained me."

"No shit?"

"No shit."

That was Detroit. Smallest big town in the world, 140 square miles and five inches deep.

Combing through Carlisle's notes, there was absolutely nothing I could see that placed Strawberry at the mansion, which is not to say there wasn't a party. But nothing suggested a cop killed her beyond the first detective's spectacular leap of logic that it had to have been a cop who murdered her since she was killed with a .40 caliber pistol, the same caliber weapon issued to Detroit police.

It was a theory that launched a thousand bar-stool conspiracies. And Detroit loves a good conspiracy. Strawberry's murder had become the city's grassy knoll.

I said good-bye to Carlisle and went back to the newsroom. I called that first investigator and confronted him with the facts.

It was the middle of the afternoon, and he sounded creaky and unstable, as though he'd been beaten silly with a feather pillow. He couldn't explain the factual discrepancies but offered me this: "To be perfectly honest, it's like an octopus's tentacles that spread all over. In Detroit, once you see it, once you connect the dots, it's obvious."

The only thing obvious to me was the people of Detroit had been duped by a loon. The mayor was a liar and a cheater, but he wasn't a murderer—at least not in the case of Strawberry it seemed to me.

I was convinced that I had the answer to the mystery of the murdered stripper. And it had nothing to do with the mayor. And that's the way I wrote it.

The story ran on the front page of the *News*. I came into the office at nine. The place was empty except for a receptionist. The light on my phone was blinking, letting me know I had a message. Maybe several. Maybe a dozen, I figured.

I threw my coat on a vacant desk next to mine, got myself a cup of coffee and sat down with a notepad to listen to them all.

There was only one. A single two-word assessment of my worldview.

"Nigger lover."

JOY ROAD

THE TELEPHONE RANG. I didn't recognize the number on the screen. I picked it up.

It was my niece, Ashley.

"Hi, Uncle Char," she said in a gooey voice. She was stoned, I could tell. Her baby-girl tone gave it away. So did the slurring. She called me Uncle Shar.

Fuck, I said to myself.

"Hey girl," I said to her. "What's going on?"

"You know how it is with me," she said pathetically. "Not much."

"Yours is a common problem."

"Yeah, that's true, but it's worse when you're a fuckup like me."

This was the place where she expected me to provide her the opening; the place where I was to ask with real sympathy and concern: "What's wrong?"

Then, according to the script, she would bombard me with her self-pity. That would give way to her self-loathing, which would end with her hitting me.

I didn't bite. I let the effort strangle in silence.

"I haven't been to your new house yet," she said finally, her voice crackling honeycomb. "I haven't even talked to you. You've been home a month now."

"Yeah, well . . . Sorry about that. Unpacking boxes and trying to get some stories in the newspaper. I don't have much time for anything else, I guess."

"How about if I come over and help you? I could watch the baby."

I ran it through my mind: If I let her over, she would stay for a week. She would watch TV, smoke all my cigarettes. Eventually, sick of looking at her and the kid howling with a diaper full of shit, I would bawl her out, giving her the pat lecture about making something of her life.

Then she would make off with my car and my liquor cabinet.

Life in Detroit had gotten tough.

Everyone was broke and if they weren't out of work, they were half out of work. One of my brothers pulled his tooth out with a pair of pliers because he had no dental insurance and was too proud to ask for the loan.

And then there was my niece. I loved her—I loved her hard—but I didn't trust her. Everybody in America has young people like that.

"We'll work out a day and then you can come over."

"You'll have to pick me up. My boyfriend totaled my car." She laughed. "He was wasted. What a loser."

Her casual, spiritless laughter worried me. Just like her mother.

My sister, my three brothers and I grew up on Joy Road, the dividing line between Livonia and Westland—two working-class suburbs about three miles west of the Detroit city limits. Our house was an equal distance from the shopping mall and the Ford plant, somewhere between the Jeffries Freeway and the dead Rouge River.

The north side of Livonia—on the other side of the freeway—was well-to-do and WASPy. Our side was populated by working-class Italians, Scots-Irish, Arabs, a few blacks and a sprinkling of Vietnamese. The sort of place where people drive American cars, not German.

It was not a ghetto by any means. Those are just the gradations of middle-class America unknown and unseen by a kid growing in its belly. Ours was a good home. A mother who wrapped her arms around us at night. Dinner on the table at six. We were taught the difference between the salad and dinner forks. We had a wall of books and some good friends. The schools, funded by the taxes from the auto plant, were some of the very best public schools in the state of Michigan. That's why my mother and stepfather chose to move here from Gary, Indiana.

But Joy Road wasn't always so joyful. Sometimes, even with all the love and the best intentions in the world, things get balled up. What happened in the 1970s and early '80s had never happened before in American life. Drugs were a scourge. You couldn't sit on the school bus without a mullet-topped greaser trying to push a bag of PCP on you. And this was seventh grade.

Divorce was another thing. Men like my stepfather were packing their bags, walking out the door and never looking back. The kids were left to fend for themselves as Mom—God bless the old girl—went off to earn the bread. Suddenly, the six o'clock dinners with Cronkite stopped.

As a consequence, I knew a lot of children who caved in to the greaser on the school bus. My siblings were among them. So were the other kids who hung around our house and ditched school while our mother was working in the flower shop on Detroit's east side. I remember a runaway named Doc who lived in his car outside our house, sleeping on Joy Road and waiting for crumbs from our table—and there were always crumbs at my mother's table. My sister's friend Carrie came to live with us for a while. It was fine with her mother, one less mouth to feed. It was fine with my mother too. And it was fine with me. She was gorgeous. And then one day, she simply evaporated. Gone. I wouldn't see her for decades. Not until my sister's funeral.

Nobody bothered to get educated. My sister and brothers and Carrie and Doc and too many others dropped out of high school, yet nobody went to work in the automobile plants. You suspected the work was too hard and the union made the work too hard to get. Two of our neighbors' fathers worked at the leviathan Ford River Rouge complex in Dearborn, on the western city limits of Detroit. It must have been terrible in there. They both killed themselves with a rope. Who knows?

Still, we had all gotten a taste of it, summer jobs sweeping the floor or working the press. It was horrible. The yellow lights, the stink of grease and oil and acid. The unblinking time clock. You walked in the door and the first thing you're trying to figure out is how to get out. If you don't know that about factory work, you don't know anything.

What our generation failed to learn was the nobility of work. An honest day's labor. The worthiness of the man in the white socks who would pull out a picture of his grandkids from his wallet. For us, the factory would never do. And turning away from our birthright—our grandfather in the white socks—is the thing that ruined us.

But even so, a high school dropout could count on the factory or the tool-and-die shops or the gas stations if he needed them. The assembly line would live forever, we thought. But like Doc sleeping out on Joy—named after Henry Joy, the president of the now-defunct Packard Motors—we thought we could live off the crumbs. Instead of working, we figured we could be hustlers and salesmen and gamblers and partiers. Work was for suckers. If anybody had told us such a thing existed, we probably would have tried to become New York bankers and stockbrokers. And I have no doubt we would have been good at it too.

Work versus The Hustle. That was the internal conflict on Joy Road, USA. My mother gave us the work ethic. My stepfather taught us that the best dollar was an easy dollar.

Predictably, the marriage didn't hold up. How could it, with the wife grinding out an honest living while the mackdaddy husband cavorted around in a green Lincoln Continental with a loaded .22 in the glove box, playing poker until all hours of the morning?

I loved the man and I hated him. He read voraciously and he gave me an affection for books. Without that, who can tell? But he also bred in me an antipathy to authority. He possessed a volcanic temper. The marriage ended when I was about fourteen, after he opened my head with a large oak spool my mother used as a candle holder. I ran and hid in the weeds on the other side of the street, blood dried on my face, looking at the house on Joy Road, hating the place. Hating it so bad I wanted to go away forever. I remember sitting there in that weedy lot thinking if I ever made $50,000 I'd be a rich man. I'd be a rich man and I could take my mother and brothers and sister away and we'd never have to come back here again.

But my sister, she ran away young. First at fourteen and permanently by seventeen. While she turned to the streets, I turned toward the classroom and the sporting field and my friends. I owed my mother that much.

Our mother, an elegant woman, militantly loyal and rabidly Catholic, worked hard in her flower shop on the city's east side—she wore herself down to such a nub. But she was still there at the sporting events, standing on the thirty-yard line in her raccoon coat teaching a young angry man the meaning of family.

When her children got lost, she went looking for them.

My brother Jimmy got lost in the blizzard of the eighties crack cocaine epidemic. He was sixteen and working and living in a crack den in Brightmoor—a notoriously rough section in northwestern Detroit. His boss was a black dude named Death Cat, the son of a successful dry cleaner. Jimmy's job was to branch out the business to the white suburban clientele, where the real money was.

My mother got wind of where he was working and drove over there. She knocked on the side door of the crack house. It was early evening and business was at full pace. She stood at the door shouting that she wanted her boy returned and if she didn't get him, she was going to call the cops.

"Yo, get that crazy bitch outta here," Death Cat ordered my brother.

My brother came to the door.

"Ma, what are you doing here?" he said, stepping out.

"Jimmy, your sister's lost out here somewhere and I'm not going to lose you both."

"Ma, are you fucking crazy? These guys'll kill you."

"Jimmy," she said with streaming eyes. "I work too damn hard to lose you kids to this city. I want you home with me now."

Wild-eyed crack heads continued to file in and out, with this little Rockwell scene playing out near the screen door.

"Okay, okay, Ma. Just go. I'll call you in a day or two," my brother remembered saying.

A week later, someone made the call for him, when rival drug boys strafed his Buick with semiautomatic gunfire. One bullet entered into the windshield at chest level and by the divinity of physics ricocheted downward and lodged in the dashboard.

That's when Jimmy, thankfully, came home.

Nicole didn't, except occasionally to steal furniture or clean herself up. And that was always a curious thing. No matter what outrage she committed, my sister was always welcomed in my mother's home on Joy Road. It was her daughter's home too, and always would be. That's what love is.

When she was clean, my sister's career consisted mostly of serving men eggs and bacon. And when she was sober, Nicky was one of the most magnetic women you could find. Handsomely built with an oval face, she had no trouble finding wholesome company.

But my sister could never make it stick. In 1986, she became a mother. Incapable of nursing both a child and a drug habit, she abandoned her daughter, Ashley, to my mother and my mother's new husband before the baby could even crawl.

My mother had had high hopes for her. We all did. Despite the fact that Nicole's demons had dragged her away from her baby girl, Ashley was lucky. She wasn't going to grow up around strange men and whiskers and dope and booze. She was going to grow up in a loving home and learn those old-generational values of self-respect and bootstrap accomplishment. She was going to appreciate art and go to college and date nice boys. With her, all the mistakes of the past generations would be mended.

But things have a way of not turning out like they're supposed to. Ashley, as much as any of us, was a spawn of Joy Road.

. . .

"So yeah, I'm staying at Grandma's," Ashley went on. "If you can come and get me, I'll meet you there."

I was home. But I couldn't bring myself to accept the responsibility of it.

"Gimme a couple days," I lied. "I'll come get you then."

"Okay," she said. She sounded genuinely happy. "I love you, Uncle Shar."

"I love you too, sweet pea."

I never did call back. I feel cheap about it because I'll never be able to fix the fact that I failed her. I locked her out. I broke the rule of Family.

EIGHT MILE

MY BROTHER FRANKIE was trying to make it work with a wife and two young daughters on a half-time job. He leased a Chrysler Town and Country minivan and took out the cheapest insurance he could—one with a $1,000 deductible. That was fine until someone tried to steal it and it cost him $750 to replace the ignition switch.

"Who the fuck would want to steal a minivan?" He laughed when I picked him up in the morning.

It wasn't funny. The $750 it cost to fix it set him back on his heels and the snowball began to roll.

Gas was $4.16 a gallon. Frankie's wife's hours got cut back. Bills started to go unpaid. Credit cards went ignored. They got behind on the mortgage. The bank wasn't listening.

Then the lease for the van came due. Give it back or buy it. He was in the red on the miles and owed $3,500 in overage. Frankie asked to buy it, but the company wouldn't give him the credit, seeing the credit card problems he was having. Frankie didn't cry.

He told the car company to screw themselves on the $3,500. It wasn't malice or dishonor. It was just the way it had to be in Detroit.

It was the least Chrysler could do for him since the company was contributing to the collapse of his neighborhood. Frankie lived two doors east of the Dodge Ram plant, which was down to a single shift since nobody could afford a truck anymore, much less a Ram with an eight-cylinder Hemi. Even the rats seemed to know Chrysler was on its last legs. They fled the plant in hordes, infesting my brother's neighborhood, nesting in his garage and under his house.

Chrysler took the van and Frankie began to take the bus to his part-time job in Detroit working as a computer guy at the art college downtown.

"What a fucking trip," he would tell me of the bus odyssey from Warren through the guts of the Detroit ghetto. He would marvel at the neck-high grass that went ignored and the garbage heaps that went uncollected. He would snap surreptitious photographs of the scene.

"I'm Rosa Parks on that bus. The only white man. You ought to hear it. It's 'nigger' this, 'nigger' that," he told me over beers at his VFW hall, a dreary joint with a keno machine and wobbly tables and people ready for the embalmer's table. " 'I'll kill you, motherfucker,' that kind of shit. Unbelievable. The city bus is how school kids get to school, and they're sitting next to a wino puking on his shoes. Or a kid's got the flu and he vomits on the bus and all the kids are laughing at him, and he's so embarrassed he gets off the bus into the cold. And his mother ain't coming to get him. And you're thinking these kids don't have a fucking chance 'cause they don't. And nobody cares."

The VFW hall was just a few blocks from Frankie's house. Having been stationed in Korea, Frankie had technically served in a foreign war and so he was welcomed as a dues-paying member. They didn't seem to mind that Frankie returned to the States without even a private's stripe, this having something to do with a hooker in the barracks and him covering for a sergeant.

When he got home, the grizzled Nam vets voted him in as an adjunct general, a nod to the younger generation. I don't know what he did in his officer capacity and he didn't get along with the rednecks so well, but the $1 beers worked for Frankie for a while and I'd go drinking with him there occasionally.

Frankie lived in Warren, just a quarter mile north of Eight Mile Road, the geographic dividing line between the black city and the blue-collar white suburbs.

But Warren isn't a suburb really; it's just a continuation of the urban sprawl. It was set up as an antidote to Detroit's increasing blackness during the war years, with Eight Mile serving as a moat. It was the home of the famed Reagan Democrats, those blue-collar whites who voted Republican because of the perceived racial slights of affirmative action. The saying in many white households then as it is now goes something like this: "If I'm gonna lose my job, at least it ain't going to a nigger."

Few whites then seemed to think much that the interests of the black working class were the same as theirs.

This blue-collar suicide seemed to shock pundits and professors and they flocked to southeastern Michigan to study working-class whites like so many zoo animals. But they shouldn't have been surprised. This was the same group of people who delivered the 1972 Michigan Democratic primary to Gov. George Wallace, the snarling segregationist from Alabama.

A cloistered rough-and-tumble place, south Warren had changed only incrementally over the preceding thirty years. It offered a nice—if unremarkable—middle-class life. If you had to live near and work in a factory on a boulevard strung with power lines, at least it came with a vacation cottage on a lake somewhere and a power boat. This is what you got if you committed your life to the machine.

Then the economy started to turn south, and folks couldn't make the mortgage notes on their discolored aluminum-sided Cape Cods. Instead of losing the house to the bank, they would either sell it to a slumlord or rent it themselves to Section 8 recipients from Detroit, who had their rent paid directly by the federal government.

Now the neighborhood was a boiling stew of white culture going broke and blacks who had known nothing but poverty for two generations.

South Warren—the part that directly touched Detroit—used to be about the Stars and Bars flag of the Confederacy flying from the flagpole in the front yard. The Dodge factory and the General Motors plant and the cinder-block mom-and-pop tool-and-die shops that supplied those factories also supplied the groceries and the fishing trips and the new car every other year. By the time I arrived in Detroit, perhaps 75 percent of those shops had died.

The industries replacing them were increasingly drug sales and prostitution. What came with those businesses were not better schools but gunshots and rusting cars and broken porches with men drinking from paper bags. Tough-looking kids hung around the playground up the street, slinging dope. Frankie started keeping his daughters inside.

Frankie had bought his house for $70,000 a decade earlier. It was an unpretentious two-bedroom with an unfinished attic on a double lot. It wasn't worth $15,000 in 2008, if it was worth a nickel.

Oftentimes, the bus home would be an hour late and my brother would sit in the cold at the transfer station near the State Fairgrounds, the wind blowing him upright.

I felt bad for my brother and I wanted to help him. But my brother is a prideful man. He didn't want a loan. He didn't want a ride. He stuck with the bus. It gave him perspective.

"It could be worse," he said. "I was standing out there one day, it was piss-cold, and the bus drivers went on a wildcat strike, but they didn't tell the kids. So you got the kids standing out there in thin coats freezing their asses off and nobody bothered to tell them."

Frankie is six-one and 130 with a pound of pennies in his pockets. He has scoliosis, an eighteen-degree curve in his spine from when he was struck by a car as a kid. It gives him the perpetual look of being bowed by a wind gust. Frankie looks raw—he wears a Fu Manchu mustache, is heavily tattooed and carries a large chip in his heart. He has an iron head and a big right hook.

A black man at the bus stop wanted his camera. Frankie looked up at him, and then at the man's friend, and then back at the would-be thief and said: "You're gonna be embarrassed for the rest of your life that you got your ass kicked by a white guy weighing a hundred and thirty pounds."

The black man walked away while his friend laughed at him. Still, Frankie stopped carrying the camera.

One night at the VFW hall, a retired cop—a stringy older white man—told a story about a black man killed on the beat. It was during the early 1970s, and the white man had just gotten back from Vietnam and was a rookie on patrol with a partner.

"We were chasing him down through an alley," the man explained. "We couldn't catch him. So I pulled out my service revolver and shot him in the back. He died.

"So they tape off the scene, and the investigating sergeant in charge of the scene walks up to me and my partner and pulls a starter pistol from an ankle holster and says, 'Okay, here's the story. The nigger pulled this cap gun, see . . . ?'"

The sergeant always wore a cap gun in his ankle holster, the old white man explained. Just in case a black man decided to run and a gun accidentally went off and struck him dead in the back. That's how order was kept along Eight Mile in the old days.

The old white man seemed blistered by the memory, like it was burning him up. Frankie bought him a drink to cool him off.

Since its founding, Detroit has been a place of perpetual flames. Three times the city has suffered race riots and three times the city has burned to the ground. The city's flag acknowledges as much. *Speramus Meliora; Resurget Cineribus*: We hope for better things; it shall rise from the ashes.

Detroit first burned in 1863, in the midst of the Civil War, when a ten-year-old white girl accused a swarthy-skinned tavern owner named William Faulkner of rape. The *Detroit Free Press* wrote at the time that Faulkner had but "a trifle negro blood in his veins." But Faulkner denied being a "negro," claiming he was of Spanish and Indian descent.

A trifle was enough for the white mob that went berserk after his conviction, putting an axe in one black man's skull and burning down thirty-five buildings. Federal troops were called in.

Detroit burned again in the race riots of 1943, during World

War II, after a group of white teenagers got in a brawl with a group of black teens. The melee quickly spread through the city as rumors of a white girl being raped by a gang of blacks fueled the mobs. People were pulled from cars and beaten; the black quarter of town was set on fire. After three days of rioting, thirty-four people were dead before federal troops quelled the violence.

Detroit burned yet again in 1967, when police stormed a speak-easy frequented by black men. A party was in full swing for soldiers returning from Vietnam. The cops attempted to arrest all eighty-two people at the west side establishment at the corner of Twelfth Street and Clairmount, turning billy clubs on the patrons and onlookers alike. Five days later—only after the National Guard and the army's Eighty-second Airborne were brought in to restore quiet—the violence ended. Forty-three were dead, more than seven thousand had been arrested and two thousand buildings had burned.

And so Detroit has the ignominious distinction of being the only American city to have been occupied by the United States army three times.

Michigan may geographically be one of America's most north-ern states, but spiritually, it is one of its most southern. During Detroit's great expansion between 1920 and 1960, nearly half a mil-lion blacks came north from the cotton fields of the South as part of what is known as the Great Migration. Detroit was seen as the Prom-ised Land, where a man could buy himself a house with a patch of grass, just as long as he had a job to pay for it. And Detroit had plenty of jobs.

Southern hillbillies also came to places like Detroit and Flint looking for unskilled factory work. The Klan in Michigan exploded in membership during the Roaring Twenties. By the end of the decade, there were estimates that eighty thousand Klan members were living in Michigan, half of them in Detroit, with other klaverns throughout the state in places like Grand Rapids and Flint.

What the black man found when he came to Detroit was de facto segregation enforced with bodily threats and restrictive real estate covenants that barred him from living almost anywhere but in the Black Bottom and Paradise Valley neighborhoods that ran up east of Woodward Avenue—the spine of the city that divides east from west. The area was vibrant with jazz clubs and black-owned stores, but it was densely packed, plagued by rats and rotting garbage and substandard housing. Consider the more than two hundred rat bites that were reported in the Valley in 1952.

Then came the urban renewal and interstate highway projects that rammed a freeway down the middle of Paradise Valley, displacing thousands of blacks and packing the Negro tenements further still.

Predictably, the city exploded. And following the 1967 riots, whites would begin their rapid exodus to the suburbs, leaving behind their homes and taking their factories and their jobs and their tax dollars with them—to places like Warren.

Five years after the riot, blacks seized political control of Detroit with the election of Coleman Young, the city's first black mayor. Vengeful, intelligent and always good for a turn of phrase, Young famously said in his 1974 inaugural address, "I issue a forward warning now to all those pushers, to all rip-off artists, to all muggers: It's time to leave Detroit; hit Eight Mile Road. And I don't give a damn if they are black or white, or if they wear Super Fly suits or blue uniforms with silver badges. Hit the road."

The remaining whites took Young's words to mean that they should hit Eight Mile Road. And they did.

Detroit reached a peak population of nearly 1.9 million people in the 1950s and was 83 percent white. Now Detroit has fewer than 700,000 people, is 83 percent black and is the only American city that has surpassed a million people only to contract below that threshold.

"The blacks wanted out of the ghetto and now the whole city's a ghetto," said the blue-haired bartender at the VFW hall, weaseling in on our conversation, assuming she had a sympathetic audience. "Young ruined that city."

Merle Haggard was playing on the jukebox. I looked at my brother, who appreciates a good bar brawl. I hadn't been to a cracker barrel like this in a while, not since the last time I'd come home for the holidays and sat at this very bar. That time, we were asked to leave because I had used profanities when I called out a local for being a phony veteran of war. Apparently cussing is not allowed in the VFW, although pretending you saw action overseas is only a minor offense.

Frankie was smiling at the bartender. "I guess that depends on who you're asking," he said with a dismissive wave of his cigarette. "And which side of Eight Mile you're standing on. Blacks might think you ruined it when you left without cleaning up your mess."

The place went silent. Except for good ol' Merle.

"We don't burn our draft cards down on Main Street . . ." he sang.

FIRE

NOT ONLY WAS the city crumbling because of sex scandal and political corruption, it was on the verge of bankruptcy. Streetlights were broken or shut off for no apparent reason. Garbage went uncollected. Sewers backed up into houses, drowning an entire block in crud. Ambulances were busted down and sometimes didn't show up for hours to emergency calls. Police cars were a decade old. Meanwhile Kilpatrick and his wife drove around in an expensive Cadillac Escalade paid for by the taxpayers of the country's poorest city.

So in an attempt to save money, the mayor was trying to force cutbacks on a besieged and beleaguered fire department. One morning, as I sat in the somnolent newsroom, listening to the silence occasionally interrupted by the occasional *tick tick* of an editor's key strokes, I read an article in the morning *Free Press* where the mayor insinuated that the city firefighters had a bum's job that consisted mainly of sleeping and eating steak, with the occasional fire thrown in to pass the time.

From my days covering Ground Zero for the *Times*, I learned who firemen were: the closest thing to cowboys that existed anymore. Imagine a man willing to run into a burning building. They had an insular culture and a way of speech and a thousand stories that few ever bother to document until calamity strikes.

Kilpatrick had made a thousand enemies in boots with his comments in the paper, I knew right then. I put on my coat and went to see the man.

Dan McNamara was the typical big-city union boss who appeared to have graduated from the kiss-my-ass school of negotiation.

"If the mayor thinks it's so easy working the back of a truck, have him call me," said McNamara, president of the firefighters' association. Silver-haired and mustachioed, he sat behind a large desk with his fingertips pressed together, pantomiming the diamond shape of a vagina. "I'll arrange it so that pussy can do some real work."

"I'll do it," I told him.

"Do what?"

"I'll tell him he's a pussy and then *I'll* ride on the back of the truck."

McNamara smiled through his mustache.

He drove me to the east side where the men assigned to the Squad 3/Engine Co. 23 firehouse work. We pulled up on a block checkerboarded with an inhabited house next to a burnt-out shell, next to an inhabited house, next to a shell and so on, something like a meth addict's mouth.

In the middle of the street were three rigs and a dozen or so fire-fighters mopping up a fire in an abandoned house that was next to a tidy little Cape Cod inhabited by an old woman.

The officer in charge that day was Mike Nevin, a balls-out, high-energy guy with a potato nose and an outrageous mullet hairdo—short in the front, party in the back. I imagined that if an ember fell on the long mop hanging over his collar, his head would ignite like a blond Brillo pad.

I could tell right away, Nevin was one of those no-bullshit, take-no-prisoners sort of leaders that men instinctively follow into combat, but by the looks of his troops' equipment—melted helmets, boots with holes, and coats covered with thick layers of carbon that made them the equivalent of walking matchsticks—these men, it seemed to me, were nothing less than soldiers garrisoned on some godforsaken front. They were fighting an unwinnable war, and it was taking its toll. Detroit was perpetually on fire. The burning couldn't be stopped.

"You did a good job, boys," Nevin told the troops. "We saved an old lady's house. Probably saved her from the homeless shelter. She invited us over for dinner."

As I was making notes, one of the firemen, a big guy with a shaven soot-stained skull, tapped me on the shoulder.

"Is your name Charlie?"

"Yeah," I said, surprised someone would recognize me in this obscure corner of the urban desert.

"My name's Dave. I went to school with your wife's brother. You remember me?"

I said I did. We got drunk someplace a long time ago. We shook hands.

"Well, welcome home. Such as it is."

"What the hell happened?"

He gave me an "if I had a nickel" shrug. "I just put 'em out, man. And there's no lack of work. That's all I know."

Nevin walked up. "So you want to be a fireman?"

"No, I just want to watch. See what you see. What happened here?"

He was holding a plastic gas can.

"Arson," he said. "In this town, arson is off the hook. Thousands of them a year, bro. In Detroit, it's so fucking poor that fire is cheaper than a movie. A can of gas is three-fifty and a movie is eight bucks, and there aren't any movie theaters left in Detroit, so fuck it. They burn the empty house next door and they sit on the fucking porch with a forty, and they're barbecuing and laughing 'cause it's fucking entertainment. It's unbelievable. And the old lady living next door, she don't have insurance, and her house goes up in flames and she's homeless and another fucking block dies."

I wrote it all down. I knew there was a story here.

A few days later, I came back to the firehouse to embed myself, like a correspondent tailing a squad of marines in an Afghanistan backwater. We loaded up on a rig and went for a tour. Also on the truck were Jimmy Montgomery, a short, excitable white man; Montgomery's best friend, Walt Harris, a burly, soft-spoken black man who moonlighted as a Baptist minister; and Jeff Hamm, who had a second career as a nurse.

It was raining lightly and near dusk. The evening had an oily quality about it. Nevin looked out the window with a vacant ten-mile stare.

"Why did I even come to work?" he said to me from the front passenger's side as we idled at a stoplight, watching a guy in a parka smoke a joint. "You know what it's like working this job in this city?

It's like those old black-and-white movie reels of Vietnam. Like those soldiers waving at the camera, like, 'Hey, Ma, everything's cool. Everything's all right.' You know? And there's a pile of corpses behind him and he's smoking a joint and playing cards. 'Hey, Ma, love ya. See ya in eight months.' I mean, it's whacked. Somebody here's gonna eat it. Somebody in this truck is going to get seriously hurt, sooner rather than later. This city's burning all day and all night long and we got shit equipment—I mean, look at these boots. And nobody gives a shit."

He put a finger through a hole in the shank.

"It's just a matter of time until somebody goes down. You know? Just a matter of time, because it can't keep up like this."

At the wheel, Harris, the minister, chuckled, then turned on a side street and was delayed by a drug deal through a car window.

"Look at this shit," Nevin continued, watching a faded crack head walk away. "Look at that guy. He's a forgotten person who's forgotten himself. It's sad. What else has he got? They talk about New Orleans and Katrina. But there's no airdrop here. There's no relocation plan or rebuilding money. They left people like him here to survive and what else has he got?"

Nevin sprang from this neighborhood. His grandfather, a Lithuanian immigrant, slapped bumpers on cars at the Packard plant. His father was born a few blocks from the firehouse and retired after serving nearly thirty years in the department. And now Nevin was working here too, trying like all the brothers in the firehouse to keep the remnants and its people from burning to the ground. "I love this place, this neighborhood, these people," he said. "I'm angry with the people in power who are supposed to lead and don't."

We turned by a Lutheran cemetery on the way back to the firehouse. An earthmover was there, but instead of placing a casket *into* the ground, it was taking one *out*.

"What's going on there?" I asked.

"They're removing the dead," Harris said without irony. "Taking him to the suburbs."

"No, that can't be true," I said. Firemen hazing the gullible reporter?

"Suit yourself," Harris said.

I wrote a note to myself on the back of the notebook to check it out later. White flight. Black flight. Now dead flight.

Harris himself had moved to the suburbs of Sterling Heights— the city north of Warren and the Eight Mile border—finding it too difficult to raise his children in the city among the people he loved. And the people in his new neighborhood—his white neighborhood—had problems with a black man moving in.

"It is too hard raising kids in the city anymore. And then when I moved up there it was sort of a 'there goes the neighborhood' feeling at first," Harris said of being the only black man on his block. "But it got better once they got to know me."

Harris turned the rig left onto East Grand Boulevard, past Kirby Street. The firehouse is located on the city's east side, near the hulking wreck of the Packard automobile plant that closed in 1956 but which nobody ever bothered to tear down. A square mile of industrial decay, scavengers had descended upon it, ushering in a marathon game of cat and mouse. The scavengers, looking for metal to sell at the scrap yard, light a section of the building on fire. After the firemen dutifully extinguish the blaze, the scavengers return to help themselves to the neatly exposed girders and I-beams that form the skeleton of the structure. From the rig, you can see the missing roofs and walls and forty-foot holes in the ground and the trees growing inside, and the whole thing looks like a gigantic, cancerous atrium.

"It's like we work for the fucking scrappers," Nevin said.

A walkway that arches over Grand Boulevard, connecting the south portion of the plant to the north, holds a marquee with missing letters, spelling out an appropriate epitaph: MO OR CITY IN U TR L PARK.

A block away is the firehouse. Inside is a perpetual pot of coffee, which the men stand around while waiting for the next run, and they don't get to the bottom of their cups before the next run comes.

The radio box bleated incessantly like a colicky sheep across a city constantly in flames.

"Ladder 16, please respond."

The response:

"Ladder 16, out of service."

Jimmy Montgomery laughed. He laughed every time he heard something like that. We went out and stood on the street corner. Everything seemed broken here: the toilet seat in his firehouse, the city government that pays his check. He stared at the house across the street on East Grand Boulevard, the one with a blue tarpaulin for a roof. He looked at the weeds. The abandoned car. The empty little factories and workingman bars and the bakery where he used to get his bread when he started on the job seventeen years ago.

Even the alarm in the firehouse was broken. And since no one from headquarters had bothered to come out to fix it, one of the boys here jerry-rigged it into some Rube Goldberg mousetrap contraption.

When a call comes to the station, a fax paper rolls out of the printer containing the directions to the fire. So someone had it rigged where the fax paper pushed over a door hinge with a screw mounted on it. The screw touched an electrified metal plate that was wired to the alarm, which completed an electrical circuit. The bell rang. Then the box bleated.

In came a call: A man has tapped into the gas main with a garden hose because he is too poor to warm his children. The hose leaks. The block explodes. They arrive at the neighborhood three minutes later. The place looks like a painting from the hand of Hieronymus Bosch, a landscape of fire and human failing. The firefighters pull the children from the flames and peel a guy's guts from the jagged window frame where he lies like an old cloth doll. One fireman gets in the ambulance with a kid, holding one hand over her eyes, the other over her shattered femur.

There is a crater where the house used to be.

"Is it ever gonna stop?" Nevin asked no one in particular an hour later through his cheap cigar, nonchalantly, as though the carnage were an everyday occurrence. "Children are dying in this city because they're too fucking poor to keep warm. Put that in your fucking notebook."

I put it in my fucking notebook.

Eight men returned to the firehouse with faces of mud, dirty and tired, and before they knew it, the box was bleating again. This time, it was a run-of-the-mill house fire in a city with 62,000 vacant homes. They jumped into the rigs and were off in seconds, barreling down Mt. Elliott Avenue. Motorists didn't even bother to move to the side. The siren had become a nuisance here.

And when the firefighters arrived at the abandoned place, what they saw was a table that had been set for supper, eyeglasses left on top of a book. The cupboard was filled with cans and cereals. It was as though the owner went out for a walk with the dog two decades ago and never came home.

It was then I began to realize who the Detroit firefighter is. He is the man holding Nero's fiddle.

It seemed to me that by virtue of the job, Nevin and Harris and their firefighting brethren were uniquely situated to witness the backward march of a great city and the fight to keep its living people from the ash bin of history.

The depth of Detroit's problems was burned into the national consciousness decades ago in the early eighties when, inexplicably, the city would burst into flames each year in a pre-Halloween Mardi Gras of arson and destruction known as Devil's Night.

There were 810 arsons reported in 1984, as Detroit became a porch light to every fire bug across the country, a tourist destination for lunatics and thrill seekers. And only now that I was home did I realize my family was a victim of them too.

My mother's flower shop was located on East Jefferson Avenue, the main thoroughfare that runs eastward from downtown Detroit out to the exclusive Grosse Pointe hamlets.

The shop sat on the lip of a black ghetto that used to be inhabited by working-class whites. The plate-glass windows of the flower shop had bars over them, and the view from the street was blocked by plants so that stickup men might not see that my mother was working alone, which she often was. She'd been held up at gunpoint several times. She stayed in that stinking spot for many years, sticking it out, making it work, struggling to feed five kids between marriages. She was one of those people who were irrationally connected to the city, until one autumn evening just before Halloween, a crazy man lit the place on fire.

He must have torched the shop for the thrill of it, because

he took nothing. The senselessness of it left my mother stunned. Why destroy for no purpose? Why burn down a building, a neighborhood, a city? She boarded up the back and stayed awhile longer until someone threw a brick through the window. She replaced it. A week later someone threw another brick through the window. Unable to get her mind around it, unwilling to try anymore, my mother turned her back on Detroit and moved her shop to the quaint, manicured and well-policed streets of Grosse Pointe Park.

I went back to the flower shop not too long ago. It was gone. Nothing but a heap of bricks and plaster. Kicking through the rubble, I found a few billing invoices with Ma's handwriting. When I gave them to her, she stared at them numbly. And then she wept.

A few days later, I was back at the firehouse, back on the back of the truck. Nevin wanted to make a point clear to me: "The people in Detroit are poor, but most of them are good. There are things going on here beyond an ordinary person's control. These people are hungry and they have no job. No possibility of a job. They're stuck here. And the assholes in charge, from Bush in the White House to Kilpatrick in the Manoogian, they're incompetent, and it's like a national sickness."

He told me about the rationing of firefighters, the fact that 20 percent of the fire companies are closed down at any one time due to the lack of money in the city coffers. The fact that they must purchase their own toilet paper and cleaning supplies. The fact that they are forced to wear aging bunker gear coated in carbon. The city even removed the firehouse's brass poles some time ago and sold them to the highest bidder.

When you ask him to think on a grand scale, he says the problem is much bigger than city hall.

"I guess when you get down to it, it's simple," Nevin says. "The man took his factory away, but he didn't take the people with him."

Dinner was served, and Harris, the minister, led the men in prayer as he always did. Then they regaled me with stories, including one about an unlucky man they removed from an electric power line, dangling there like a human piñata. He'd tried to cut down the live wire and sell it for its copper.

Even the firehouses themselves were not untouched by thieves. Recently the men here cooked a supper of steak and potatoes, but a call came over the box before they could eat it. When they returned, they found that their dinner had been stolen, right down to the green beans. The canned beans and coffee creamer were gone from the larder, and so was a pickup truck belonging to one of the men.

A few days earlier I watched as a deranged woman set fire to an abandoned house. As the firefighters worked to put out the blaze, the woman crawled into the fire truck and tried to drive away. The firefighters radioed police dispatch.

The response came: "No cruiser available."

They covered her in a coat and sat on her until two arson investigators came and took care of her.

We hadn't finished our supper when the Rube Goldberg alarm sounded again. And again, the men jumped into their bunker gear and into the rigs.

The fire was a few blocks away. The house was empty and unoccupied, the last one left on the block. There was a tractor in the vacant lot across the street. One of the firefighters explained to me that a farmer had turned the tumbledown neighborhood into a hay field. There were large cut piles of it everywhere among the tall grass.

As the firefighters were unrolling their hose, a group of four men arrived in a minivan with video and still cameras. They had gotten to the fire before some of the engine trucks and they wore jackets with patches from fire departments all across the country, which led me to believe they were from headquarters or the union hall. One guy was eating a candy bar.

"You firemen?" I asked with my notebook out.

"Something like that," one guy answered creepily.

I asked Walt Harris, the minister, who they were.

Harris looked over at the tall hay on the next block, at the older black people standing on their porches in their bathrobes. Harris looked at the white men wannabes and their fire patches.

"They probably set the fire since they got here before us," he said. "They come, they take a motel and they drive around with a scanner waiting for a fire to go off," Harris explained to me. "It breaks your heart. What's happening here, it breaks your heart. Every one of these guys here will tell you that he'll give you everything he's got to help the people of this city. He'll give his life if he has to. It breaks your heart."

I looked at the douche bags with their cameras and their New Jersey fire department patches. They needed their asses beat down. Where were the police? Where was anybody?

MONGO

THE WAY I saw it, I had mailed Kilpatrick a great big valentine with the dead stripper Strawberry story. With daily revelations about women and pay-to-play schemes within his administration, it was the closest thing to good press the man was going to get.

Now it was time for payback. Kilpatrick owed me lunch and an interview at the very least, and I called his people to say so.

But he was hiding in his badger hole and he wasn't about to come out, I was informed.

"What's in it for him?" asked his spokesman, James Canning, over coffee in the eastern wing of City Hall. We were sitting in a window across the street from the Renaissance Center, the world headquarters of General Motors. It was a workday morning, but the buildings and the streets below were empty. My eyes went from a panhandler and settled on Canning, a young white man who had the unenviable task of standing before the news cameras and lying that it was business as usual for Mayor Kilpatrick who was hard at work saving the city.

"What's in it for him?" I echoed back, summoning my best big-city big-shot-reporter indignation that I'd honed for a decade at the *Times*. "I'll tell you what's in it for him. If he *doesn't* give me an interview, I'll kick his ass every day up and down Woodward. That's what's in it for him."

Canning looked sour, like I'd just pissed in his coffee cup.

"Where'd you come from?" he asked. "New York, right?"

"Yeah. New York."

He nodded, then scribbled a name and number on a business card. "Here, call the reverend. He can speak on the mayor's behalf."

I looked at the card: *Rev. Horace Sheffield.* I put the card in my pocket.

"And lunch?"

"I'll ask."

"Tell him I'll pay."

Reverend Sheffield had a community center on the far west side of town, walled off from the ghetto he served by a pike fence and an electronic gate. The son of a UAW icon, Sheffield operated in part on public contracts and grants from city hall. Since the feds were crawling up Kilpatrick's ass, that spigot of money had dried up. When I later called him, he complained to me that his cell phone had been shut off and he was in danger of missing his mortgage payment.

His center was drab and ill lighted and as I walked in toward the reception desk, I stopped and looked at the classroom where a half dozen kids were slouched in chairs, doodling or groping one another. According to the signage, this was the life skills program for at-risk youth, ostensibly where that money from city hall went.

I signed in at the desk.

"The reverend is on a telephone conference," the attendant told me, and I took a long, cold seat.

I studied the civil rights photographs on the wall—the well-dressed black men at the union rallies and dinner banquets—and I realized how little I knew about the history of Detroit, its race and labor record, the rough-and-tumble machinations of Detroit black—and for that matter, white—power. I was wearing a tie, but I had neglected to shave and I noticed a small hole in the knee of my blue jeans.

I really had no specific questions for Sheffield, because I knew nothing insightful to ask. I simply wanted to stare big-city politics in the face, study the knickknacks and doodles on its desk.

Then power walked in the door: a short, stocky, smooth-skulled black man wearing a full-length leather trench coat accompanied by a tall, large, well-dressed sidekick. I had them pegged for members of the Nation of Islam.

The bald man in the trench coat gave his name to the receptionist: Adolph Mongo.

I may not have known much around town, but I knew *that* name. Adolph Mongo. You couldn't avoid it in Detroit. Mongo's technical title was consultant. But he had other names: the political hit man, bomb thrower, assassin. These were titles of prestige.

Mongo cut his teeth in the Coleman Young administration in the early eighties, working as a deputy director of communications. A former marine and itinerant newspaperman, Mongo came from a family that was powerful in the black underworld of Detroit's heyday. According to him and his brothers, Mongo's uncle was a bootlegger and numbers runner, his great-auntie the madam of a brothel. Mongo's dead older brother moved heroin and cocaine. So naturally when Young took control of the city, the Mongo clan insinuated itself into a place at the table.

Mongo's older brother Larry became something of a consigliere to Young, and so when Adolph came knocking, Young put him to work, and his experience in the Young machine taught him that Detroit politics was an insular and imperious world.

Once, Robert Mugabe, the African revolutionary who would later become president of Zimbabwe, came to Detroit to receive the keys to the city. Mayor Young made him wait an inordinately long time for an audience.

Mongo remembers it this way: an underling stepped into Young's office and said, "Sir, you've got Robert Mugabe, the freedom fighter, sitting out there."

To which Young replied: "Fuck Robert Mugabe. This is Detroit."

Detroit indeed. We once gave the key to the city to Saddam Hussein. And never took it back.

Watching a retinue of Young sycophants take the plunge into prison, Mongo decided to strike out on his own. "It was crooked even then," he would tell me later. "I wasn't willing to do what they asked. I wasn't willing to risk my freedom for a two-thousand-dollar suit."

Still, he was connected, and so Mongo became a political consultant. You could hire him to strategize for you—or you could pay him to keep his mouth shut or he would hammer you mercilessly. Mongo knew where the back doors were.

Mongo had beat on Kilpatrick in the lead-up to his reelection campaign, making the local television and radio circuit calling Kilpatrick a pansy and a mama's boy. Instead of fighting him, Kilpatrick simply hired Mongo for $200,000—proving to many that he was indeed a pansy and a mama's boy.

With Kilpatrick down double digits in the polls, Mongo came up with a now infamous back-page "lynching" ad that ran in a special edition of the *Michigan Chronicle*, an ad commemorating the life and death of Rosa Parks.

The ad drew a comparison between a historical photograph of black men hanging from a tree and the media's treatment of Kilpatrick. It worked. Kilpatrick stormed back from the double-digit deficit to victory. Mongo knew the number-one rule of politics: win.

Black politicians pretended he didn't work for them. White politicians suffered the same amnesia. But they sought his advice and they drank with him during the off years of the election cycle. I couldn't have cared less. He was what politics really were around here. It was my job to know him.

"Adolph Mongo?" I said, standing up and offering my hand. "Charlie LeDuff, the *Detroit News*. I've been meaning to meet you."

He gave me the eye. "Goddamn motherfucker. Dressed like that? I thought you was a junkie or some shit."

He shook my hand, introduced the large, well-dressed man as his younger brother Skip and took a seat next to me.

"You that motherfucker that wrote that stripper story," he said. "Good fucking story. I try to tell the mayor, he's got to work the media better. He can beat this thing if he looks like he's in charge. But he ain't listening. He's a talented guy. But he's ignorant. Politically ignorant. Ignorant of history. He don't read. You know he doesn't have a book in his office? Not a fucking book in the shelves. Ain't that some shit?"

The receptionist interrupted: "Mr. Mongo, the reverend will see you now."

Mongo got up to go, took a few steps down the hall, turned and asked me: "You wanna come in?"

"With you all?"

"Yeah, motherfucker, with us all."

I went along.

Sheffield sat imperiously behind his desk, a man in excess of three hundred pounds. He was a large presence in the community. Besides his social work, he preached on the east side of town and did a lot for the people, often pulling money from his own pocket to pay for funerals. He was another who talked the race game—despite the fact that his father was black and his mother was white. In Detroit, we all talked the race game. It is a way of life.

As we walked in the door, he looked at Mongo and then at me.

"I invited him," Mongo said. "He's all right." I took a seat in the back. Sheffield was planning a run against Rep. John Conyers—the aging, barnacle-like fixture in the U.S. Congress. Conyers had served more than twenty terms in the House and had presided over the collapse of his district—including Highland Park—where he did not even bother to keep an office.

Highland Park, the birthplace of the Model T, was an industrial hamlet wholly surrounded by Detroit. Today, little is there. It is poor, black, burned down and so tough that even the Nation of Islam moved its mosque away. The saying goes that suburbanites don't go to Detroit and Detroiters don't go to Highland Park.

Conyers was weak. If only someone with connections to the churches would man up and run against him, he could be taken out.

Sheffield was smart, I could see that. He viewed the chessboard and was almost convinced he was the man to put Conyers king down, and he hired Mongo to do his groundwork.

Conyers's district was gerrymandered into a strange racial stocking that also included some working-class white communities.

"The rednecks would vote for a fucking pink donkey before they'd vote Conyers," Mongo said. "You're black, but Conyers is the face of everything they hate."

But Sheffield was getting pressure from D.C.: Charles Rangel, the longtime congressman from Harlem, had called that very morning and asked Sheffield to bow out, and Sheffield, a product of the political machine, was considering it.

"I have to think about it, Adolph. There's a lot to consider here. I've got a lot to lose."

"Oh goddamn, Horace, you ask me to do this shit and then you act like an old white woman. You think about it then," he said with exasperation. "Call me when you decide."

Mongo and his brother left. I decided to leave with them.

Mongo turned to me at the door, near the room where the students were now sleeping with their heads on the tables. "Did you learn anything?"

"I'm not sure," I said. "He seemed pretty worried about an opportunity that seemed there for the taking."

"It got decided a long time ago in Detroit," Mongo said. "The city belongs to the black man. The white man was a convenient target until there were no white men left in Detroit. What used to be black and white is now gray. Whites got the suburbs and everything else. The black machine's got the city and the black machine's at war with itself. The spoils go to the one who understands that."

"So we're standing in a moment of history?" I asked.

"That's right," he said. "And you're going to find out, if you stick around, that a lot of the people holding political power nowadays are some bizarre incompetent sons-a-bitches."

"And what about the reverend back there?" I asked, pointing to Sheffield.

"Fuck it," Mongo said, shaking his head at a lost opportunity.

LIPSTICK AND LAXATIVES

I BEGAN TO understand just how bizarre Detroit politics could be when I met Monica Conyers, the high-strung city councilwoman, for a cocktail at a local jazz club in the early summer.

The youngish and voluptuous wife of the doddering congressman, Conyers had come to city politics under the banner of being a Conyers.

Her campaign commercials had the murky production quality of bad porno films and looked as if they'd been shot through a shower curtain. Still, they were simple and traded hard on her husband's name as a civil rights warrior.

"Join the Conyers family as we fight to take back Detroit from those who put self-interest above your interest," she cooed, dressed in a form-fitting blouse that highlighted her ample cleavage. "Detroit deserves better."

Detroit chose Conyers, a political novice whose thin résumé included failing the bar exam four times. And Conyers got to work before she was even sworn in. Her first order of business was to pummel a woman in a barroom brawl after the woman complained about Conyers chatting up her man. The woman left with a black eye as big as a tea saucer.

Just in time for my arrival in Detroit, Conyers—in her capacity as a trustee on the city's pension board—threatened to shoot one of Mayor Kilpatrick's aides who rubbed her the wrong way.

"I'll have my brothers fuck you up," she shouted at the man, according to the police report and news accounts. "I'll get a gun if I have to, and I got four brothers who'll whup your ass."

Conyers denied that she threatened the man. She said he started it first. She filed a complaint against him after he filed one against her.

Monica was my kind of woman. As least as far as the reporter in me goes. She was a self-absorbed, self-serving diva. A honeypot and a loudmouth who let a bit of power go to her id.

It didn't matter to me if she spent tens of thousands of dollars on overseas trips paid for by the city's pension fund. It didn't matter to me if she mishandled the business of the poorest citizens in the country. It wasn't my problem. It was my job.

She typified the politician of the current American landscape. An overfed buffoon who fattened herself at the public trough while the ribs began to show on the gaunt body politic. And in that capacity, she was nobody special. Chicago had its Governor Rod Blagojevich. Newark had its Mayor Sharpe James. San Diego had its Congressman Duke Cunningham and Youngstown, Ohio, had its Congressman James Traficant.

Clowns for sure. But Monica's makeup was better. She was the perfect political caricature wrapped up in a real human being.

And one thing about clowns. Clowns sell copy.

I started keeping notes on her. Monica was fascinating. The big-mouthed girl from a broken home—her father had a record for breaking and entering, her brother for robbery—Conyers was susceptible to violent outbursts. She was a drunk in rush-hour traffic, a wreck in the waiting. I could have been related to her. I waited for the moment and Monica delivered.

One day, after showing up to council chambers looking tired and wan, her hair a mess and pulled back in a rubber band as if she'd just rolled out of bed, Monica flew into a rage when she was gaveled down by the balding council president, Kenneth Cockrel Jr., over some unimportant business.

She shouted at him. She intimated that he beat his wife. She called him "Shrek." Twice.

Cockrel threatened to adjourn the meeting, to which Conyers shrieked: "Do it, baby! Do it!"

He did it. The scene made the six o'clock news. People printed T-shirts.

I had to get myself a piece of this. I called Conyers's political adviser—a rakish con man named Sam Riddle who seemed to play the role of Clyde Barrow to her Bonnie Parker and accompanied her on her lavish trips paid for by the pension fund. I had met him once previously for coffee, at which meeting he told me: "The only difference between Detroit and the Third World in terms of corruption is Detroit don't have no goats in the streets."

Riddle answered the phone. He complained bitterly about a colleague of mine who wrote an unflattering story about him taking trips on the pension board's dime.

"She's a fucking bitch, and I don't talk to the *News*."

"You'll have to take that up with her," I told him. "Her sins aren't mine."

"Oh yeah?" Riddle shot back. "Go fuck yourself."

He hung up.

I called back ten minutes later, thinking it an appropriate amount of time to have gone and fucked oneself.

"Look," he said, before I could even say hello, "I don't even work for that crazy bitch Monica Conyers anymore. She gives me gas. I don't want to put up with her bullshit anymore. I'm too old. Do you know what I'm saying? Do you?"

I didn't know what he was saying, but I said that I did.

He called himself her pimp, except for the fact, he said, that he didn't like standing in the night air.

"Anyway, can you reach out to her?" I asked. "I'd like to do an interview."

He thought a moment. "Would it be front page?"

"If it's good," I said. "I can't see why not. I'll even make a video for the Web site."

"Let me see," he said. "I'll call you back."

Not only did Conyers agree to do it, baby, she also agreed to my bringing along a group of schoolchildren who would ask her questions about her behavior in the council chambers, all of it to be videotaped.

The children arrived at the council chambers with their prepared questions in hand. They took the seats of the politicians behind the big oaked arch. At first, they cowered before Conyers, who sucked the air from the chambers with long, empty bromides about her march from squalor to law school to the chapel with a powerful congressman to the position of president pro tempore of the Detroit City Council. She insisted the children call her by that title: City Council President *Pro Tem*. A fancy way of saying runner-up.

Finally, Riddle stepped in and asked the children about the Shrek incident.

"Anybody have an opinion on that?" he asked the kids. A thirteen-year-old girl, Keiara Bell, asked Conyers if she felt she'd been disrespectful toward the council president and the city itself.

"What do you mean by that?" Conyers asked with a sneer.

"You're an adult," Bell lectured. "We have to look up to you."

"Absolutely," Conyers replied. "You've never gotten angry with someone?"

"Yes, but we're kids. We're looking on TV, and, like, this is an adult calling another adult Shrek? That's something a second-grader would do."

Conyers could barely contain her anger. Her eyelids flared, her jaw clenched.

"Now you're telling me, young lady, what I should have and should not have done?"

"Well, you're an adult," Bell countered. "Sometimes people need to think before they act."

Not surprisingly, the video made its way around the world via the Internet, and Conyers became yet another symbol of what was wrong in Detroit: murder capital, arson capital, poverty capital, unemployment capital, illiteracy capital, foreclosure capital, segregation capital, mayoral scandal capital—and now Monica Conyers capital.

Her negative publicity boiled for a month: the *CBS Early Show*, the front page of the *Wall Street Journal*, even the local television stations. None of it credited to the dying *Detroit News*.

Suddenly, Conyers was everywhere for the wrong reasons.

Naturally, Monica wasn't happy and wanted to tell me. In person. We arranged to meet.

As I drove to my rendezvous with Conyers at a cocktail lounge off Eight Mile Road, I decided to stop off at Keiara Bell's home and say hello to her family.

I hadn't seen Keiara since the "Shrek" taping, which had made her a YouTube darling and an example of what is good in Detroit. I drove through the crumbling neighborhoods on the city's west side, where she lived.

When I had left home—back in the early nineties—Detroit was still the nation's seventh-largest city, with a population of over 1.2 million. Back then, Detroit was dark and broken and violent. Murders topped six hundred a year and Devil's Night—the day before Halloween when the city burst into a flaming orgy of smoke and shattered glass—was at its height.

Studying the city through the windshield now, it wasn't frightening anymore. It was empty and forlorn and pathetic.

On some blocks not a single home was occupied, the structures having fallen victim to desertion and the arsonist's match. I drove blocks without seeing a living soul.

I stopped by the Bells' home off Livernois, once known as the Avenue of Fashion. They lived in a Tudor alongside other grand Tudors that surrounded a park with long, unkempt grass and a broken drinking fountain. I knocked on the iron gate that sealed the front door. The Bells weren't home. They'd taken their rattletrap Cadillac and gone around the way to sell candy from the trunk,

since the only other candy to be bought within a five-mile radius
was at the liquor store.

A dead sycamore that had snapped in the wind was lying in the
street.

Harry Bell, the family patriarch, praised God when I called him
on his cell phone to find out where they were. I asked about the tree.
He said the sycamore had fallen on his car a week ago during a heavy
rainstorm and smashed it. He'd been asking the city for months to
cut the dead tree. He called the city to come clean up the timber.
But it was still lying there like a corpse.

"The car still works," Harry told me over the phone. "Great is
He. God works miracles."

Harry was a typical Detroiter: unemployed part time, full of
God and finding hope anywhere he could get it. *At least the car still
works. Praise Him!*

I drove around the corner to meet up with the family. They
were in a neighborhood of blown-out, windowless houses mixed
with others that had neatly manicured lawns. Harry grew up on this
block.

His wife, Marsha, waved wildly and ran to give me a hug. "Heya,
Mister Charlie!"

I blanched. "Mister Charlie" is an old slang term from antebel-
lum times, a name given by slaves to their white oppressors.

"Please, I told you, Marsha. Don't call me Mister Charlie."

I shook Harry's hand. He looked ill, and he was ill, suffering
from obesity and hypertension and high blood pressure. He was my
age but looked ten years older. He used to work in a fish house, but
was too sick to stand anymore. I worried about him and how his
family would get along without him and his steadying influence, if it
should come to that.

"Where's the kid?" I asked him. He pointed.

Keiara was in the front of the car, head down and sullen.

"What's the matter, Kei?" I asked, sliding into the backseat.

She shrugged her shoulders. "I don't know," she said. "All the attention, I guess. It's got me thinking. I'm ashamed. I'm ashamed to be poor. And I'm ashamed to live here. And I don't know if I'm ever going to get out. I just want to move away."

"Where would you go if you could move out? The suburbs?"

"No. I wouldn't really fit in there," she said. "Maybe the country, way far away, where there's nobody to bother me. And it's just a little farm and I have my family around me and nobody else."

"That's a good dream," I said. "That's my dream too. It'd be nice to have you for a neighbor."

She smiled, and I smiled back, knowing the odds went against her. Half of Detroit kids don't even make it through high school, and of those that do, half of them are functionally illiterate.

Keiara was an honor student despite it all. The secret to her success, her mother said, was to lock her in the house at all times, except for the fifteen hours a week they spent at church. If any kid was going to get that farm, it was going to be Keiara.

It was growing late. I had to meet Conyers, so I said good-bye to the family, promising Harry I would call the city in my capacity as a reporter to see if I couldn't shame someone into removing the dead tree blocking the street.

"Good-bye, Mister Charlie!" Marsha shouted as I pulled away.

I headed west and drove up Linwood Avenue. I remembered the street. I often delivered funeral flowers from my mother's little flower shop to the black churches that lined the boulevard. Usually, the arrangements were gaudy casket sprays and urns stuffed with purple and orange pompons. Men would always greet me at the back door, dressed in dark funeral suits of varying exoticness: black, lavender, sometimes blood red or tangerine orange.

I drove past the Shrine of the Black Madonna, the pan-African Christian church that set itself up in the 1960s as the militant alternative to the oppressive white version of Christianity. In the Shrine's version of the passion, Christ is a black man.

The church boasts thousands of members, if not worshippers. It delivered the vote that made Coleman Young Detroit's first black mayor, in 1973, and has since been the wellspring of black political power in the city. Politicians like John and Monica Conyers still paid reverence. The county sheriff was the nephew of the Shrine's founder, Jaramogi Abebe Agyeman, formerly known as Albert Cleage. The executive ranks of the fire department and Kilpatrick's chief of staff were worshippers, as were various local commissioners and Kilpatrick appointees, recipients and perpetrators of no-see, no-bid municipal contracts and favoritism.

In fact, Kwame Kilpatrick himself was raised in the church, his parents having met there in the 1970s.

The founder, Cleage, had threatened to burn the rest of the city down following the devastating riots of 1967, and by the looks of things, he hired the job out. The church's colonial steeple was collapsing into the street, the paint was peeling and some leaden windows along the nave were boarded up. The buildings surrounding the church to the west and north were charred and broken, like a forgotten row of tombstones. I found it curious that the center of black power in the city should look so awful and dilapidated.

A few blocks farther on was the New Bethel Baptist Church,

founded by the Reverend C. L. Franklin, who was a great friend of Martin Luther King Jr. and the father of soul legend Aretha Franklin.

Reverend Franklin made his bones as a Detroiter and died as many do. In 1979, he was shot during a home break-in. He suffered a painful death. He was placed on a respirator but did not succumb to his wounds until six years later.

That church too felt drab and sick, the sidewalk littered with garbage, the building sandwiched between vacant lots, a gas station and a liquor store.

Before it was New Bethel, the church had been the Oriole Theater, once the headquarters of the Church of Universal Triumph, the Dominion of God Inc. That congregation was led by a man known as Prophet Jones.

During the 1940s and '50s, Jones was one of the most successful showman-evangelists in the country, one of the few black preachers who broke the color barrier and was broadcast nationally by the white-controlled media. The *Saturday Evening Post* dubbed him the "Messiah in Mink."

Bejeweled and flamboyant, Jones was something of a Little Richard of the cloth. He was said to have four hundred suits, four thousand bottles of cologne and four Cadillac cars, with a separate chauffeur for each. His congregants, both black and white and mostly Southerners alienated by Detroit's culture of concrete and steel, were happy to keep the Prophet in riches. He preached from a golden throne and was said to be able to hear God in his right ear, on which he wore a diamond earring to better help the reception.

Prophet Jones's main theological precept was that come the year 2000, all living humans would become immortal. In order to reach the millennium, Jones decreed that "women should wear girdles, long enough to keep the stomach and buttocks from protruding." He also stipulated that they should wear red nail polish in the evenings and take laxatives once or twice a week.

The fall came quickly for the Prophet, who in 1956 was charged with making homosexual overtures to an undercover police officer. He beat the rap, but his reputation never recovered. Jones did not come to realize his own prophecies. He died in 1973, the year Coleman Young was elected mayor.

As the sun set, I arrived at Baker's Keyboard Lounge, a jazz club on Livernois near the Detroit side of Eight Mile Road, the place my wife's parents used to frequent in the eighties.

The bar was full, despite the fact that the joint stank like a sewer pipe. Conyers was seated in the back, near the stage.

It was early summer, and she sported a brassy, low-cut cream-colored top with a tight skirt, exotic stockings and high heels. The way she was stuffed together, it looked like she was wearing a girdle. She was definitely wearing red nail polish.

I ordered bourbon and soda. She ordered tea and lemon and a Caesar salad and a cup of soup. She said she was fasting, trying to clean her intestines out and lose weight.

We made small talk.

"You know what I'd like to do after politics?" she asked.

"What's that?"

"I'd like to design brassieres for plus-size women," she said.

"I'm sure there's a big future in that," I said, amused.

She batted her eyelashes coquettishly and crossed her legs with a grand gesture, leaning one side of her hindquarters sweetly toward me.

"The congressman and I don't spend much time together any-more, but that's our marriage and it works for us," she cooed.

I ordered another.

That's when Monica got to the point. She complained that I had set her up. I assured her it was not a setup, that Keiara Bell had her own mind and that it was doing Conyers little good to be complain-ing in the press that a thirteen-year-old was disrespectful of her rank.

"Okay, can we speak as adults?" I asked.

"Go 'head then," she answered with a barracuda smile.

"What the fuck is the matter with you?" I asked. "You're fighting with a kid."

The smile vanished. Her teeth appeared. I was ready for the nails and a drink in my face.

"She was a plant," Conyers hissed.

"She was not a plant, she was right," I said. "Look. If I were you, I would go on camera and say the girl reminds you of yourself, that growing up in this town, you have to develop a thick skin. You say that she has taught you something about civility and that you are proud of her."

It was good, free advice. Conyers should have taken it.

Instead, she smiled coyly again. She straightened her shoul-ders, leaned over the table and patted my chest. Her hand wandered down my torso and lingered on my testicles. She gave a gentle little squeeze.

"Are you wearing a wire?" she asked.

"No," I said, momentarily stunned. "That's a roll of quarters. But I'm flattered. I really am."

This couldn't be happening, I thought. Girdles and red nail

polish and intestinal cleansing and bar fights and sewer pipes and wiretaps and eternal life and decay all around. It was insanity. It was outrageous. It was a reporter's wet dream. Where the hell was I?

I paid the bill and left.

The sign outside said DETROIT CITY LIMITS.

Trains, Planes and Automobiles

IF THE MASTERS of the universe in New York are the moneymen of Wall Street, then in Detroit they are the automobile executives. We did not question the decisions they made concerning business. The union man might have pushed him for an extra buck, but the car executive knew what was what.

Until we found out he didn't.

The realization came on September 15, 2008, as gasoline was selling at $4.24 a gallon and the Dow Jones Industrial Average tumbled 504 points. That's when Lehman Brothers—the august Wall Street investment bank—announced it was bankrupt.

The bankruptcy set off a chain of events that showed the country was not in the midst of a business cycle. It was an epoch. Americans were living on a bubble of credit and stock market gambling, and when the marker came due, they could not pay.

International currency markets panicked, access to credit dried up, Wall Street teetered and the Big Three—unable to sell their gas-guzzling hounds—were on the verge of ruination.

By October, with the bankers lined up in Washington with their hats in hand, the national debt clock in Times Square froze at $9,999,999,999,999.99

It had run out of numbers.

The Wall Street collapse was fueled by the trading of exotic bits of financial paper. But Detroit was different. We made cars—not paper and false promises. What happened? How did Detroit—the most iconic of American cites—become a cadaver?

Detroit's slide was long and inexorable. You might blame it on white racism and legal mortgage covenants that barred blacks from living anywhere but the most squalid ghettos.

You might blame postwar industrial policies that sent the factories to the suburbs, the rural South, and the western deserts.

You might blame the city's collapse on the 1967 riot and the white flight that followed. You might blame it on Coleman Young—the city's first black mayor—and his culture of corruption and cronyism.

You could blame it on the gas shocks of the seventies, which opened the door to foreign car competition.

You might point to the trade agreements of the Clinton years that allowed American manufacturers to leave the country by the back door.

You might blame the UAW, which demanded things like near-full pay for idle workers, or the myopic management, who instead of saying no took their piece and simply tacked the cost onto the price of the car.

Then there is the thought that Detroit was simply a boomtown that went bust, a city that began to fall apart the minute Henry Ford began to build it. The car made Detroit and the car unmade Detroit. Detroit was built in some ways to be disposable. The auto industry allowed for sprawl. It allowed a man to escape the smoldering city with its grubby factory and steaming smokestacks.

Detroit actually began its decline in population during the 1950s, precisely the time that Detroit—and the United States—was at its peak. And while Detroit led the nation in per capita income and home ownership, automation and the beginnings of foreign competition were forcing automobile companies like Packard to shutter their doors. That factory closed in 1956 and was left to rot, pulling down the east side, which pulled down the city.

By 1958, 20 percent of the Detroit workforce was jobless. Not to worry, the city, rich with manufacturing revenue, had its own welfare system—a decade before Johnson's Great Society. The city provided health care, fuel, and rent and gave $10 every week to adults for food; $5 to children. Word of the free milk and honey made its way down South and the poor "Negros" and "Hillbillies" flooded in by train. If it wasn't for them, the city's population would have sunk further than it did.

Even the downtown train station—the Michigan Central Rail Depot—was ill fated from birth. Three weeks after it opened in 1913, Henry Ford announced the $5 workday, causing the ascension of Detroit and the inevitable bust of the train in America.

People came from Poland, from Ireland and from the sharecroppers' shacks of Mississippi. The American middle class was born here.

And the Michigan Central Rail Depot has been set upon by vandals. The mahogany banisters have been looted, as have the copper wiring, the marble walls. In a city full of ghost skyscrapers, the depot is Detroit's *Flying Dutchman*, its gravestone, a mocking symbol of its lost greatness. On a clear day, you can see straight over the river to Canada, right through the windowless building.

. . .

But whatever the reason for the nation's collapse, you couldn't blame a Detroiter for thinking it all revolved around him.

And so on November 19, 2008, the Big Three executives—Rick Wagoner of General Motors, Alan Mulally of Ford and Robert Nardelli of Chrysler, along with Ron Gettelfinger, president of the United Auto Workers—arrived in Washington to beg for a handout. Bailout backlash had not yet erupted. But when the executives from the Big Three took their seats before Congress, people caught on to the concept. Cars. Everybody understood cars. Greedy Executives and Lazy Unions. Who didn't understand that?

Sitting before the Senate Banking Committee and receiving a withering grilling, the auto chiefs showed just how incompetent they were.

When Sen. Bob Corker of Tennessee, known as "Senator Nissan" because of the large Japanese auto plant in his state, asked the executives what they planned to do with the $25 billion they were asking for, the executives didn't have an answer.

"I just want the numbers," Corker said.

After some mush-mouthed ramblings, Wagoner lamely explained that they really didn't have a plan and that they were basically going to divide the money up according to the market share of each company.

With $12 billion, Wagoner said, "We think we have a good shot to make it through next year."

They were laughed out of the conference room.

They were sent away empty-handed and told to come back in two weeks with a plan. They had come to Washington in private jets. The fact that they had better come back by automobile was an unspoken commandment. The Dow plummeted 445 points.

Watching the spectacle inside the *Detroit News*, the editors and reporters who had built the paper's credibility on automobile coverage were stunned. Had Detroit's industrial prestige slipped this far? I wasn't surprised. Of course it had. And so too had the respect for the working-class life. I learned that lesson when I was a cub reporter at the *New York Times*. There was a strike in the mid-nineties at an auto-parts plant in Flint, Michigan. There was a story in the paper that day about bum union guys spending their strike time shopping and touring around the lakes in their power boats, like it was a sin to have a power boat.

"Since when is it bad to have a boat and make good money?" I asked a *Times* editor with a weak chin and a big brain. He put his palm to his nose and said: "Those people had about this much fore-sight. They should have seen the writing on the wall and gone to college."

"If we were all poets," I said to him, "we'd starve on words."

Adolph Mongo knew it too. I got a call from him just as Rep. Barney Frank was lecturing the Car Guys on how to run a business.

"Shiiiiit," Mongo cackled. "They went up to Washington think-ing they were the executives of the Big Three. Turns out they were nothing but Detroit. They don't realize that Detroit is a code word for nigger and they ain't nothing but niggers anymore. Incompe-tence ain't exclusive to the black folks in this country."

Mongo was right. Incompetence wasn't a black Detroit inven-tion: Wall Street had taken the world's financial structure to the edge. The White House had us involved in two wars of incompe-tence paid for with a credit card. The Big Three couldn't keep their books straight. California was drowning in $150 billion of debt. Tim-othy Geithner, soon to be the new treasury secretary, didn't pay his taxes. There was not one Detroit Democrat involved in any of that.

. . .

The Big Three executives, who had been so unceremoniously booted out of Washington in November, returned to the capital in December with a more specific plan, which had now jumped from $25 billion to $34 billion. And they didn't fly the corporate jets this time.

Ford and General Motors executives made a big deal of the occasion by driving to Washington in their hybrid vehicles. Mulally of Ford came in an Escape SUV hybrid. Wagoner of General Motors was chauffeured in a Chevy Malibu hybrid.

Poor Bob Nardelli of Chrysler. The pickings were slim. Chrysler, known more for the styling of its bodies than for its technological savvy, sent Nardelli to Washington in an Aspen Hybrid SUV, about the only "green" thing Chrysler had to offer. Problem is, it was a terrible vehicle and unreliable.

Despite being partially powered by a battery, the Aspen ran on a V-8 Hemi and got less than twenty miles to the gallon. The charging system was flawed and difficult to service.

His driver was Mike Carlisle, the homicide detective who had retired in disgust from the Detroit Police Department just a month earlier.

The media was invited to snap bon voyage photographs in Detroit, which they dutifully filed. What they did not see—and what Carlisle later told me—was that there were two engineers tailing Nardelli at a discreet three-mile buffer, carrying laptops and a trunk full of tools in case the Aspen broke down. Even Chrysler didn't trust their products.

For a second time things didn't go well in the capital for Detroit's Car Guys—who mercifully arrived without incident. Sen. Richard Shelby, from Alabama—whose state is host to the Korean Hyundai,

Japanese Honda and German Mercedes-Benz assembly plants—grilled the executives with joyous hostility as they sat before the Senate Banking Committee.

"Did you drive or did you have a driver?" he asked. "Did you drive a little and ride a little? And secondly, I guess you are going to drive back?"

For the second trip in a row, the executives got nothing and were sent back to Detroit. The Dow plummeted 444 points that day.

Leaving the Capitol building, Nardelli climbed back into his unreliable $50,000 SUV for the ten-hour return drive home. But they had not even cleared the Lincoln Memorial when Nardelli, according to Carlisle, instructed him to drive to the airport, where the corporate jet was waiting.

Carlisle drove the Aspen back home to Detroit.

On December 15, President Bush, not wanting the collapse of the auto industry as another black mark on his legacy, extended a $17 billion bailout to GM and Chrysler.

The Dow closed down 26 points that day, and Chrysler announced that the Aspen Hybrid SUV would no longer be built.

SCREWED

THEY ARRIVE AT work at 7:25 A.M., and many of their cars are rusting buckets of crud. Except for the boss's. The boss drives a Volvo.

Walk in the door at the screw factory and the first thing you notice is the enemy—the time clock. Then you notice the stink of oil vapors and solvents. The dispiriting yellow light. The slippery floors. The caked and peeling walls.

The workers don't want to be here. The liquor bottles in the weedy lot out back told part of the story.

I watch the poor mopes taking the last drags of their cigarettes before the work bell rings. The cutting fluid and other oils have permanently stained the skin under their nails. And that damn lousy smell stays with them.

I couldn't take my eyes off their bad skin, made worse by grinding dust and dirt caked in their ear folds, eye corners, noses and hair. I see their skin pockmarked from the metal shavings that they probably have the wife pull out with tweezers each night while they drink a can of beer. I used to work in a place like this as a kid. Almost everybody who grew up here spent at least some time in a factory like this.

You would smell these oils and fluids in the shot-and-beer joints that lined the industrial boulevards—Ford Road, Plymouth Road, Five, Six, Seven and Eight Mile Roads. The men hunched over the rail, the grease patches in the small of their flannels, oil in their ball caps, Bad Company or the O'Jays cranking from the jukebox. The clacking of pool balls. Greasy hamburgers. Cheap whiskey.

I remembered it all as I watched the hollow, cornered faces staring at the time clock like they wanted to smash its teeth out. I remembered it all in five seconds.

The workers punched the clock at precisely 7:30 A.M., not a minute later, since otherwise they'd be docked fourteen minutes, and nobody in America works fourteen minutes for free. A quiet resignation settled over them as the roar from the screw-grinding machines revved up. Want it or not, they needed to be here. After this place, there was no place. Not in today's America.

This machine shop may be the next wobbling domino in the collapse of the American manufacturing sector and the struggles of its blue-collar workers. There were at least seven shops nearby that were available for lease.

The screw factory was in an industrial section of Garden City, north of Ford Road, about three miles west of Detroit and about two miles east of where I grew up, near the Westland shopping mall. Westland is a working-class city, and the people there fully embrace their consumer culture. As far as I know, Westland is the only city in the world that renamed itself after its shopping mall.

But as it is with most things around here, the shopping mall is on the rocks, rundown and made more dismal by the empty storefronts surrounding it and the vacant lot where the Quo Vadis theater once stood. We used to sneak in the fire door and watch movies all afternoon and into the night.

My brother Billy and his wife, Kim, were working at the screw factory. Billy was running up on middle age, with thinning hair and a widening middle, his days as the good-looking player on the wane. A high school dropout, he had no education to fall back on.

Still, Billy's a semibrilliant guy, great with numbers. Billy made $70,000 shuffling subprime mortgages for Quicken Loans before the real estate crash—and he would only go in three days a week.

Quicken was one of those mammoth mortgage brokers that sold a ton of subprime loans and quickened the American economy into the toilet. Billy used to work in an office and wear good suits. He would call himself Bill.

Now Billy was living the nightmare of every suburban white guy—working in a hellhole, standing next to a retarded fellow who's also making $8.50 an hour, counting and cleaning screws. The retard, it turns out, is better suited for the job because the retard can shut it down, turn off his mind.

For Christmas, Billy got a piddly bonus of $43.80 and was evicted from a house he wrote the mortgage on. Also gone were the suits, the expense account, the three-day workweeks.

At least he had a job. Before the screw factory, he sat around for months, unemployed, playing video golf all day, ashamed when his three kids would walk in the door from school and see him sitting in the exact same spot as when they left in the morning.

"When Kim came home and told me that this place had a job opening, I'm thinking, Great! A factory job. I'm thinking union. I'm thinking fifteen bucks an hour and bennies!

"Nope. Eight-fifty an hour. Dude, I made more than that in high school. I wanted to cry, but whatcha gonna do?"

Then my brother recited the new battle cry of a generation: "I'm just glad to be working."

My brother was standing at his workbench in sagging pants and the oily ball cap, where he aired out screw nipples made in China with a hose, cleaning them and repackaging them for American customers who don't want to know they're made in China, only that they come cheap. Billy wasn't wearing a respirator or eye protection. It was lunchtime. He was drinking a cup of coffee with powdered creamer and a lot of sugar. The place was silent.

There was no health care offered here. What constituted a dental plan came from a toolbox. That is, my brother attempted to take out an abscessed molar with a pair of pliers. The molar snapped below the gum line.

What happened to us, I asked him? How in the world did it come to this?

"Man, you won't fucking believe it," he said. "Dude, people here refuse to work. I mean, the boss asks them to work an extra couple of minutes, and they're like, 'Fuck that, I'm outta here.' They hate me here because I actually work. You know? It helps pass the time. I don't mind letting it be known that the place is a shit hole and I don't belong there. I've got a real disdain for the place. They know it. So they hate me. 'Cause I remind them they're stuck here. I can't blame them, though. You can't when you get a look at this place up close.

"I'm like, yeah! And then I get the rude awakening when I walk into this mausoleum. One fucking guy has been here thirty years, walking around with his chest swelled out, saying, 'I make nineteen dollars an hour.'" Billy cackled. "Nineteen fucking dollars an hour. Then the boss cut it by two dollars, and the guy stays. The boss really has him by the balls. It's all he knows. This and deer hunting. Me, I don't care. I ain't dying here. They all know I feel this way. I don't hate them. I just hate this fucking place."

He absentmindedly stapled another box, even though he was on break. The box had a stamping that read: PARTS MAY BE MADE IN UNITED STATES, CHINA OR TAIWAN.

"One day, the boss asks me to clean the fucking toilets," my brother said. "Can you believe that? Clean the fucking toilets? I'm in there kicking shit around. It's filthy. These guys here are animals. The john stinks like hepatitis. I mean, I'm no Harvard scientist, but I'm used to a pretty good life. This shit is humiliating. But I need the job, so I swallow my pride and go in.

"I'm kicking shit around trying not to breathe out of my nose, and I open a stall and there's graffiti in there. It says 'Fuck hard workers.' Just unbelievable. That's everything you've got to know about working America right there. 'Fuck hard workers.' The point is, no American wants to work.

"Go ahead, go in there. The right stall, above the toilet roll."

I went in. He wasn't kidding. The locker room smelled like a rotting stag. Like a rope of frozen urine stabbing you up your nostrils. Right stall, soiled toilet paper thrown on the tiling like they do in Mexico so as not to clog the pipes. Here, I figured, it's just laziness. There was the graffiti: *Fuck hard workers.*

I walked back to his work station and he was laughing.

"Man, at least my family's eating. You know? But I'm not used to this. I shouldn't be here. I'm a salesman. I'm a good salesman. There's nothing I can't sell. But there's nothing to sell right now. I was asked to go back to Quicken, but I'm thinking, fuck that—the hours are too long and the work is borderline criminal. I figure I'm here doing my penance. Quicken used to have three thousand loan officers when I was there. Now I hear it's about two hundred. You know what I mean? At one point in this country, when that shit was the rage, one in ten adults was employed in the real estate business. What's that tell you? We were all living a lie and we all knew it.

"I sold bullshit mortgages. Subprime. Negative amortization. Neg ams, they're called. I did. And I'm sorry about that. A lot of people got fucked. I got fucked. I got evicted from a house I wrote the mortgage on. Sheriff locked me out and locked a bunch of my shit in. CDs and clothes and furniture. No big deal. I can replace it all. At least the kids weren't in there."

He laughed.

"How did it work?" I asked.

I'm only now getting smart about what I should have been smart about a long time ago. As a reporter, I think I've failed. I forgot about the smell of places like this. They don't have those smells in the bars where newspaper people go.

"Okay," my brother said. "For instance, let's say you want a $100,000 house and you've got nothing down and you want to pay one of these neg am interest-only mortgages. I'm trying to push you into that at, say, 5 percent."

"Make it 7 percent," I tell him. I'm not sure if this is a well-rehearsed bullshit story of his. I want to test his math skills.

"Okay, 7 percent then. So a neg am loan allows you to cut the 7 percent to 3.5 percent, with the 3.5 tacked onto the back end of the loan. Get it? So you're paying $290 a month with no principal being paid."

I used a calculator. He was just $1.67 off.

"And that other $291 is being added to your principal. So, say, after five years, you've added . . . $17,500 to the principal."

I typed it in. Bingo. Right on the money. "Man, you could have been something if you'd gone to college," I said.

He laughed again. But his heart wasn't in it.

"Anyway, you now owe \$117,500 on the house. After that five years, once the house gets 90 percent loan-to-value—that means you're getting close to getting underwater—the bank 'recasts' the loan and now flips you to a full am, which means you pay an old-fashioned mortgage, which is principal plus interest on \$117,000. You now have a thirty-year loan at 7 percent. Plus you have to buy the mortgage insurance because you don't have anything down, which puts you somewhere at \$900 a month. Your payments have more than tripled overnight. A \$200,000 house is now costing you \$1,800 a month and we both know the guy was never making that kind of money.

"We bullshitted and rehashed his qualifications to get him into that house. People without jobs were getting houses. I heard stories of dead people getting loans. We had cons in the office working as brokers. No joke. It was all a hustle.

"You get the guy in a loan and then you call him three months later and tell him the loan he's in—the loan you got him in—is a bad deal, and you sell him a different loan. It was a shell game. And the company pushed us to do it. We were making six points on every deal. Six! And nobody cared, 'cause everybody was getting what they wanted for free.

"Okay. So the house isn't really worth what you're paying. You're over your head. 'But you're gonna flip it,' I tell the guy. 'Houses are increasing in value by 10 percent every year nationwide,' I tell him. 'You can't lose. Take that 3.5 percent and put it in the stock market, which is going crazy. You're rich.'

"But I know he's not putting it in the market. He's an American—he's going out and buying a Cadillac and snorting dope. I wrote hundreds, maybe thousands, of these bullshit loans to people who shouldn't have gotten them. I helped a few people, sure. And I helped a lot of people help themselves.

"Then the real estate market starts tanking. The job market is tanking. Gas is going up past four dollars a gallon. And Wall Street's doing who knows what the fuck they did with all this bad paper I pushed. I thought it was a problem. We all did. Now we know for sure. We all walked away from the obligation. And we're screwed. Real estate's not coming back for a long, long time. It was too inflated."

My brother pointed to the guy working at the next table over. "Go talk to him," he said. "That guy's actually paying off his debt. He's an honest guy, I'll give him that. But he's sort of retarded. He's too dumb to know he should just walk away from the debt."

The man working next to my brother is named Mike. A functional illiterate, he earns $8 an hour but takes home about $75 a week. Up to his neck in house payments on a house that was no longer worth what he owed, Mike decided to pay the bank instead of walking away.

Why? I asked him. A lot of people are walking out on debts.

"A lot of people do, but I don't," he said. "If everybody walked away on what they owe, where would we be?"

He was potbellied, sported a poor Moe Howard "Three Stooges" haircut and was missing his lower plate of teeth. But he wasn't complaining about the slow pace of a national dental plan. He was worried about his job.

"What happened?" I asked him as he fiddled with the same bolt I had seen him fiddling with for fifteen minutes.

"Happened where?"

"Here, in America. What happened to the economy? What happened to this screw shop?"

"Well," he said with gummy exasperation, "a guy used to make plastic cars, see. Then they found a guy someplace else who can make forty plastic cars. But the guy that used to make the cars still likes the car. He wants to buy one for his son for Christmas. So he buys one with a credit card. But he don't have no money to pay for that credit card. After a while, the man with the credit card wants to get paid, but the guy that used to make the plastic car don't have no money to pay it."

He stopped abruptly and shrugged his shoulders.

"That's what happened, I guess."

The illiterate understood it. And he told it as well as the *New York Times* ever did.

I walked back to my brother's bench.

"How you feel about what you did?" I asked my brother. "I mean, you dropped out of high school, you pimped bad loans to people. You blew all the money you made, and now you're making $8.50 an hour counting screws same as the guy over there who can't read."

"I look back and I feel broken," he said glumly. "I mean, I'm managing to squeak by. I've got three kids, so I'm happy. I've got people who love me, and we're eating and got a roof over our heads. But when I was making real money, I blew through the dough. I rent a house now for $800, when I was renting an apartment then for $1,500."

His wife, Kim, walked up and handed him a soft drink.

"Thanks, babe. Anyway, when you have it, you don't think about it, because it's going to last forever. At least I did. See, Char, I've got a salesman's mind. Most of us do. Salesmen and gamblers. That's why there's a casino in every town now. I guess what I'm saying is, I blew it."

"Imagine what we could do with that money now," Kim said and walked back to the office.

Billy paused, his mind running.

"Being stuck here. Being stuck here is the problem," he said in an echo.

The lunch bell rang. The machines revved up somehow, by some unseen hand.

"Well, recess is over," Billy said. He fired up his air hose, which hissed like a serpent.

The King Is Dead

By EARLY FALL, it was apparent that the feds had been laying more wire in Detroit than the cable guy.

Leaks of snitches and news of plea deals and grand jury testimonies emerged almost daily, and Motown became hypnotized by a widening corruption scandal.

Kilpatrick had his problems with the text messages and dead stripper, but now they were compounding tenfold with the feds listening in on almost everybody with business before the city.

It began with a Greek who held lucrative contracts at Cobo Hall, the city's decrepit convention center on the Detroit River. He told the feds that he made illegal payments of nearly a half million dollars to Kilpatrick and his father to get the concession stands. The Greek eventually pleaded guilty to tax evasion and got off with probation.

Working off this information, the feds began tapping phones and wiring cooperating witnesses.

Paranoia ruled the day. Worried that the feds had bugged their offices, some politicos were taking meetings at the International House of Pancakes or on downtown street corners. One councilwoman was using her granddaughter's cell phone. Players were going through phone numbers like they were Chiclets.

Suddenly you couldn't get ahold of anyone.

Kilpatrick and Monica Conyers and a dozen other municipal movers and shakers were in the crosshairs of the FBI for accepting bribes in exchange for their support on a billion-dollar sewage contract.

Details leaked out of the grand jury room about Councilwoman Monica Conyers and her clandestine meetings in fast-food parking lots where she took envelopes stuffed with cash. Apparently Conyers, it seemed, was a big fan of the fish fillet sandwiches on white bread.

Feeling the heat one muggy morning, Conyers and a group of city council members stood in chambers and prayed for divine intervention. God must have been listening. Lightning struck the building, crippling it for a week.

While the feds were building a RICO case against Kilpatrick, he was charged by the Wayne County prosecutor with perjury—for lying under oath about fucking his chief of staff, Christine Beatty.

While lacking meter and polish, the fire and passion in their electronified love sonnets must surely rate with those of Elizabeth Barrett and Robert Browning.

> Christine Beatty to Kwame Kilpatrick—"Baby, if I was with you right now, I would sit you down, get on my knees in front of you. I would pull myself up to you and gently suck on your ear lobe and come around kiss you so passionately, then . . ."
>
> K.K. to C.B.—"PLEASE TELL ME MORE!"

C.B. to K.K.—"Then I would take off your shirt and kiss you down your neck and suck on your XXX. After that I would take off your pants and lay you down on the bed. Then . . ."

K.K. to C.B.—"MY SHIT IS SO HARD ALREADY."

C.B. to K.K.—"Then I would climb on top of you and start kissing you on the top of your head, move down to your face, then gently move to your stomach and gently lick around your belly button! Then . . ."

K.K. to C.B.—"DAMN . . . I LOVE THIS!"

C.B. to K.K.—"Then I would move my way down XXX and gently slide it into my mouth and move it in and out until you feel like you're inside of me and you're asking to be in me! Then . . ."

K.K. to C.B.—"SHIIIT!"

C.B. to K.K.—"Then just when you're about to come, I would take it out of my mouth and climb back on top of you and slide it deep inside of me! I would then begin to slowly ride back and forth on top of you. Then . . ."

K.K. to C.B.—"DAMN CHRIS!"

C.B. to K.K.—"Then I would pull your chest to mine while you're still deep inside of me and kiss you so passionately while riding you! I would then ask you to gently grab my ass and you would put your finger in just enough to make beg yo—"

K.K. to C.B.— "Don't STOP! PLEASE."

K.K. to C.B.—"I'm ABOUT TO COME RIGHT NOW!"

C.B. to K.K.—"Then I lay on my side and you lay behind me and pull me so close to you and I say 'I Love You So Much' and you say 'I Love You Too' and kiss my neck so soft. And then we pull up the covers and go to sleep and wake up in an h—"

K.K. to C.B.—"HELL YEAH! CHRRRRISSS! HOW DO
You FEEL?"

C.B. to K.K.—"First tell me how youuu feel!"

K.K. to C.B.—"NO NIGGA! You 1ST."

All this . . . their salaries, the phones, the cars, the chauffeur, the Kleenex, paid with the taxpayer dime.

Kilpatrick concocted an interesting legal strategy. I call it the Poltergeist defense.

Kilpatrick acknowledged that the text messages were made on his city-issued cell phone. But he insisted he didn't type them. It must have been the Ghost of Christmas Ass who tapped out the randy messages while the phone lay idle in Kilpatrick's pocket.

He hired a bevy of million-dollar consultants and lawyers, but it is apparent he heeded little of their advice. Although he was barred from leaving the state as part of his bond, he took a day trip to Windsor, Ontario—forgetting it was in another country.

Strike one.

When two sheriff's deputies went to the mayor's sister's house to serve a subpoena, the police encountered Kilpatrick there. Kilpatrick stormed out of the house yelling, "Get the fuck out of here!" and pushing one of the cops, a white man by the name of White, off the porch.

He then turned to the other cop, a black woman, and shouted, "You, a black woman being with a man with the last name White, you should be ashamed of yourself!"

Strike two.

Until then, the governor and attorney general of Michigan had stood on the sidelines, not wanting to confront a black mayor who just might evade the eight felony charges with a rogue O. J. Simpson–type juror.

But after he pushed the cop, the full weight of the system came down on Kilpatrick. The governor began removal proceedings. The attorney general began criminal proceedings.

Kilpatrick was hauled into court. The Hip Hop Mayor stood before the judge, choking back tears, his lips quivering.

"I apologize immensely . . . I am asking your forgiveness . . . I apologize to the citizens as well, but mostly to you."

What a pussy. Strike three.

The judge sent him to jail for the night.

Shit, I thought, standing there in the courtroom, watching Kilpatrick blubbering. What a big bitch. My sister had done more nights in jail. Hell, even I had.

Hip Hop my ass.

Out of moves and out of friends, Kilpatrick took a plea deal—four months in jail, a million dollars restitution and resignation of office.

Kilpatrick appeared on television and gave his resignation speech to the people of the city. He wore a garish tie, something like the old paisley drapes in a seventies bachelor pad. His wife wore a matching dress.

I watched the speech from a corner seat at Mosaic, the power players' watering hole in Greektown. The bar was packed and eerily quiet as Kilpatrick spoke. He took credit for a long list of things he never actually accomplished, among them municipal financial stability and the demolition of abandoned buildings.

You could hear the ice cubes tinkle as the players silently calculated their next moves. In the end, Kilpatrick was only a temporary hiccup. After all, when a king falls, the kingdom still remains.

The deputy mayor, drinking white liquor, shook his head when Kilpatrick proclaimed in all earnestness, "You done set me up for a comeback."

"Awh shiiiiit," someone said from the corner. It was Adolph Mongo. "Shiiiiit."

Good old Mongo. The inebriated uncle at the funeral shouting all the things people wished they could say.

"Goddamn," he cackled, his voice box one part Redd Foxx, one part cement mixer.

"Who told them to put on the matching tie and dress? They look fucking ridiculous. That's what you get for a million dollars in consultants? The guy fucked it all up. The king is dead!"

Mongo spied me in the corner, gave me a sober nod and then pretended I wasn't there. I paid my tab and slipped out the side door.

GONE TO THE DOGS

FRANKIE DIDN'T CRY when, as a boy, I hog-tied him with a belt to a tree as the cars drove by on Joy Road. As he hung potato-sack style, a group of teenagers jumped out of their car and beaned him with snowballs.

Frankie didn't cry when he was hit by a car, breaking his body forever. Frankie didn't cry when his daughters were born. Frankie didn't cry when he got laid off from Ford. Frankie didn't cry when the FOR SALE signs popped up in his neighborhood like so many horse thistle weeds.

But he was crying now.

I left the newsroom and drove over to see him. He was wearing a knit cap and a sweatshirt, looking for a soft piece of earth in which to bury his massive golden retriever.

"What the fuck happened?" I asked.

"It was the dog food," he heaved.

"What do you mean it was the dog food?"

"I looked it up on the Internet. It was the dog food. Poisoned shit from China."

He wiped his nose on his sleeve. I looked around his gray neighborhood. Somebody had stolen the aluminum siding off the abandoned house next door.

This place called Detroit wasn't interesting to me anymore. It was breaking my heart. It was driving me insane. A whole generation of people relegated to the garbage pile. I hugged my brother.

"Poison shit from China. How much is a man supposed to fucking take?" my brother sobbed. "They killed my fucking dog."

I stood with my hands in my pockets as he dug a hole in the cabbage patch, the only soft spot in the dead of winter. It was directly beneath his neighbor's window, which didn't matter so much now that the neighbor's place was foreclosed and vacant.

Frankie put stones on top of the dog so the wild animals couldn't dig him up and cart him away.

Ghosts in the Attic

"Walt's dead!"

"What? Who is this?"

"It's Nevin." Mike Nevin. Sergeant Mullet over at Engine 23. He was crying.

It was one of those lifeless, slate-gray mornings, and I was standing at the upstairs window in my home. I could see the Detroit Zoo water tower from my window. Kwame Kilpatrick's name had already been removed from it, but I could still make out the ghost of its outline.

"Hello, Charlie? Walt. He died two hours ago. A fucking house fell in on us this morning. Goddamn it. A little piece-of-shit house. One of them mousetraps. I had him in my arms. Jesus Christ. Anyway, we're over at the engine house. I thought you'd want to know."

"I'll be right over."

I lingered at the window, staring at the water tower, considering the name. Kilpatrick. What did it matter? One asshole gone, another takes his place and the shit goes on and on.

I jumped into my pants and kissed my wife. She was still sleeping and I startled her awake.

"What's the matter?"

"Walt's dead," I told her. "I got to go to the firehouse."

"Walt the fireman? Oh my God."

I had taken her and our daughter over to Engine 23 on more than one occasion, and we had grown fond of the men there. They were a fraternity of doers, and I admired them for that. I like being around men who accomplish something. It makes me feel a little bit better about being a guy who makes his living typing up clever things other people say.

"Tell them I'm so sorry," my wife said. "We'll pray for them."

I drove to the firehouse fast. The roads were empty. No one was on the way to work.

I had seen Nevin and Walt Harris—the firefighting Baptist preacher—just the day before. I had stopped by the firehouse for lunch. It had been a long time, as I'd been banned from all Detroit firehouses after I wrote my first story about Nevin's crew criticizing the mayor's office for its neglect of the department and its firefighters. But rather than accept the chronicle of their complaints and try to improve the situation, the city reprimanded Harris and Nevin and the other men who appeared in my story and hauled them downtown to give statements.

Everything Harris told me then turned out to be true now, including his death. The culture of lying about Detroit's problems went from the mayor's office to the ministers' pulpits to the no-name bureaucrats in uniform. No one wants to admit they live in an archeological ruin. That's why a house of firemen complaining about the decay were hauled to HQ.

Nothing had changed. Their pants and boots still had holes in them, the fire alarm at Engine 23 was still a jerry-rigged alarm clock, they still had to buy their own toilet paper and the city still burned.

Yes, Walt was right when he talked about people removing their dead from Detroit, just as his prophecy had been right that one of the men from Firehouse 23 was going to die.

Being a Baptist minister, Big Walt always gave the invocation before chow. And the men, loving Walt more than God Himself, dutifully lowered their eyes. The last prayer of Walt Harris was a good one: "God, look over these good men and return them to their families."

Above him, over the firehouse dining table, a teeny-bopper movie played on the television set with cheerleaders in tight sweaters pulling each other's hair out in the high school cafeteria.

I laughed out loud at the ridiculousness of it, and Harris looked up with an arch of his eye and laughed too. Then he kicked me in the shin under the table.

"Shut the fuck up, Charlie."

I ate the chicken fried steak and went home.

Eighteen hours later he was dead.

The street around the firehouse was crowded with fire engines and work trucks. The mourning had begun and, as is particular to the fraternity, it was something of an Irish wake, with distant relatives from all around the region dropping in to give their hangdog condolences. A few rookies were made to stand out in the rain to make sure nobody broke into the trucks or stole the aluminum ladders, which brought a good price at the scrap yard.

Inside the house, it smelled of cigar smoke and weak coffee and it was mostly silent except that Jimmy Montgomery was screaming, "What a complete fucking waste. For what? For what? Some dump of a fucking house? No. No. No."

The commanding officer, Lt. Steve Kirschner, stood in the corner looking on with the pallor of a sickly walleye.

I had learned about firemen. I had learned about them over the long dark days following the massacre at the World Trade Center on September 11, 2001. I had gone to dozens of their funerals, and I profiled Squad 1 in Brooklyn over the course of a year, a firehouse that had lost half its men that bad morning.

I learned that when one of them dies, the Irish comes out of the rest of them whether they are Irish or not. A firefighter is Irish by culture even if he is a black man, and there were plenty of them here. The firehouse is one of the few places in Detroit that is integrated at all. The blacks run the department, but its soul will always be Irish. And the Irish don't handle outsiders very well. Especially reporters. Especially in death. Even if one has been invited to the wake.

I had learned in New York to stand in the corner and wait to be acknowledged. So I poured a cup of coffee and waited. The men of the house had broken down Walt's bed and assembled a memorial from his bunker gear before the clock had struck nine. It would stay there as long as the house did, along with the statue of a Dalmatian and the swordfish and the American flag over the busted toilet seat and the portraits of men gone by.

A raggedy man with patchy facial hair from the neighborhood walked into the death scene, begging change. The rookie gave him a couple of bucks and a cup of coffee and kindly told him to fuck off.

Nevin watched, a Swisher Sweets cigar burning in his hand.

"You okay?" I asked him.

"This place is making me sad."

"Yeah, me too."

"Let's get the fuck out. I'll take you to the house where Walt died."

He gathered up Montgomery and Jeff Hamm, the fireman-nurse who tried to resuscitate Harris on the way to the hospital, and Verlin Williams, who was also pinned down by the collapsed roof.

Williams was an odd duck, older than many of the men in the department because he had served twenty years in the Marine Corps before moving back home to Detroit. As a boy growing up in the city, Williams would gravitate to the local firehouse, where he scrubbed and washed the engines. It kept him straight and out of trouble, and his life's dream was to serve in the department.

That is, until he got into the department.

"Now all I want to do is go out West and retire as a cowboy," he said as we rode over to the house in the fire engine. "Think of that. Spending your days breaking horses in the wide open spaces. Far away from here. Yeah."

I didn't have the heart to tell him there really weren't cowboys out West anymore. Let him have his dream. Every sucker's got to have one.

I looked out the back window and saw a reporter from the *Free Press* and his photographer tailing us uninvited.

We drove past the hulking wreck of the Packard plant, a square mile of dead factory. After a half century of rot, it still stood as a disgraceful reminder of our great past and sordid present. Its founding president was Henry B. Joy—the man who built the first coast-to-coast highway and the man for whom my Joy Road was named.

Now all that was left of his empire was a ruin that burned at least once a month, usually from the torches of scrappers. A shotgun row of houses stood directly across the street from it. Houses with children growing up inside them.

We passed more houses with blue tarpaulins for roofs and weedy lots and burnt-out cars and children. Plenty of children. Sweet Jesus, too many children.

The house where Walt died was no different from the rest of them in this east side swath: an abandoned blue and green bungalow on East Kirby Street. An arson reward poster was tacked to the door and cans of juice and beans were sitting unopened on the dining room table.

This being Detroit, the men responding to the blaze went into the house to look for people. In this city, crumbling houses are often occupied by drug addicts, the homeless and even families with children struggling to survive.

This time, there was nobody home.

As the firemen were snuffing out remnant embers in the attic, someone heard timber snap. And then the roof collapsed.

"He was right behind me," said Hamm, pointing to the spot. "He was right next to me. I don't know why I'm here."

It took a few minutes to find Harris because his homing alarm failed to sound. It failed because it was defective. Because that passes for normal here. Defective equipment for emergency responders.

Harris died not because he was burned or because the timber broke his bones. He died of suffocation, unable to breathe from the weight of the roof. If the alarm had only worked.

Harris was pronounced dead before the sun had risen.

"Goddamn," Nevin spewed, standing in the damp exposed attic.

I remembered the prophecy Walt Harris had given me six months earlier at a house fire: "Every one of these guys here will tell you that he'll give you everything he's got to help the people of this city. He'll give his life if he has to. It breaks your heart."

The men fell silent. There was only the sound of the rain.

Then I heard a mechanical click.

I spun around on my heels. It was the photographer from the *Free Press* stealing a little photograph of the scene.

The next morning, on the cover of the *Free Press* was a photograph of Verlin Williams, the would-be cowboy, reenacting his death-defying escape from the caved-in roof.

I took my daughter to the funeral. Firefighters came from all over—Chicago, Toledo, Canada, the Detroit suburbs. What struck me was the shitty condition of the Detroit equipment, the shining suburban stuff next to the banged-up, dented Detroit rigs.

Nice speeches were made. "He was a hero," said fill-in mayor Ken Cockrel Jr. "It was his brand of heroism that will never be forgotten."

It was bullshit, and everybody knew it. Criminals ruled the streets. Christ, Cockrel himself had the gutters stolen off his house for scrap metal.

Firefighter Wes Rawls had his car stolen at the memorial service the evening before. It was the third time he'd had his car stolen. One of those times, Rawls was attending an anger-management class.

Walt was put in the ground, and as quick as that, the hero went forgotten by the city.

I got a call from one of the men in the firehouse the following weekend.

"We're gonna burn it."

"Burn what?"

"The house."

"What the fuck are you talking about?"

"The house where Walt died. It's still standing."

"It's still standing?" I said, incredulous. In New York, a firefighter dies in a house, the thing gets torn down in hours. But I had to keep reminding myself, this place wasn't normal.

"Nobody gives a fuck," the firefighter said. "It's becoming a shrine, like at one of those places where kids die. There's stuffed teddy bears and bullshit stapled to the house. We don't want that shit. This ain't Disneyland. We want it down. We want it fucking gone. That's what they would do in New York."

The pain in his voice frightened me. He was violently rational.

"We've got it prepped. The holes are cut in it. We just pour some gas on it and watch it go."

"Don't do it," I told him. "Don't. Don't become one of them."

The prospect of a firefighter dedicated to saving a city ravaged by arsonists crossing the line into criminality, even if it was for the right reason, horrified me.

"We don't give a fuck anymore," he said. "Eventually, we all become one of them. We're gonna burn it."

"I'll be back to work on Monday," I told him. "Just wait. Please, just wait. I'll make some calls. I'll try to get them to tear it down. If they don't, you can torch it then."

"Would you do that?"

"Yeah, I'll do that. Just don't do anything stupid."

"All right, we'll wait."

I went straight to the firehouse that Monday. The black bunting commemorating Walt's death had been ripped loose by the wind and hung over the bay doors like a hangman's noose. No one was there. Out on another call.

I drove over to Kirby Street. Not only was the house still standing, but just like I'd been told, it was decorated with T-shirts and wilted flowers and a teddy bear, like at those street corners where a teenager has been gunned down. There was a sign that read: PERSON WHO SET THIS FIRE IS A MURDERER AND COWARD.

The fire had indeed been ruled an arson, making Walt's death a murder. And yet the thing still stood.

I knocked on a neighbor's door.

"This is the second time they set it on fire," a woman told me in her kitchen doorway. There were three children playing behind her. "They lit it on fire a couple years ago, and the city never did nothing about it the first time, and if they had, then maybe . . ."

I was scribbling in my notebook.

"Who you, the po-lice?"

"Reporter."

"You gonna get that house torn down?" asked her husband, who had joined her in the doorway.

"It'll get taken down one way or another."

"I would much appreciate that. It's a hell of a place to raise your babies."

"I bet," I said.

"Sir, you'd win that bet."

I drove back to the office and started working the phone. The building authority, the mayor's office, the demolition department. Hell, I even called FEMA. Nobody returned my calls.

There was no one in charge of the city anymore.

I eventually reached Councilwoman Sheila Cockrel, the step-mother of the interim mayor, who was more knowledgeable about the inner workings of the city than anyone I had met since I had come home to Michigan.

The process of tearing down a building is a long and tedious one, filled with red tape and greasy palms. In fact, Cockrel told me, the city of Detroit had recently been awarded a $23 million federal grant to demolish abandoned houses like the one Harris had died in. And yet the city council voted to spend just $14 million on demolition while funneling the other $9 million to politically connected ministers for their "block programs."

I told her the firemen were threatening to burn the house down.

"Tell them the house will be down by eleven A.M. tomorrow," she said. I didn't know how she was going to do it. And frankly, I didn't care. "You just made a thousand friends, ma'am," I told her.

It was a cold, sunny morning, a Thursday. My car wouldn't start, so my wife dropped me off at the house where Harris died. Matt Labash, the writer for the *Weekly Standard*, was in town writing his own elegy for the city and we had made plans to link up there.

The neighborhood was inaccessible, with the fire engines and news trucks and the motorcycles of the Axe Men, a crew Walt rode with, clogging the streets. Only in Detroit would the demolition of a house, a single straw in a haystack, draw such attention. It felt decent.

Sheila Cockrel was there. The battalion chiefs. Neighbors. Even Adolph Mongo was there at my invitation. He looked ill at ease, as though someone might recognize him and run him off the block with a shotgun. He had worked for Kilpatrick, after all. And it was safe to say there were no fans of Kilpatrick here.

"I hate this shit," Mongo said as we shook hands. "Look at it, this city is a motherfucking wreck. It just hurts me to look at it. I'm gonna get the fuck out of here."

"Stay," I said to him. "It's your city too."

I watched the newspeople interview Cockrel, the firefighters, even Mongo. I watched a local reporter parade around as if she were in charge of the morning's itinerary. Where had she been for the last decade? Something went badly and she swooped in on it like a vulture, feigning outrage and calling the community to action. It was all so pathetically obvious to me because she was behaving exactly like me and every other reporter I knew.

So I made no more paper notes. I just wanted to see the thing come down. Soak it in. Victories are few here. But it felt good. It's a feeling I'd rarely had as a newspaperman. A feeling that the work can actually be of some benefit to somebody.

When the bulldozer began to tear at the roof, people cried. And when the last wall came down, they applauded. I shook hands with the men of Engine 23, gave Montgomery and Kirschner and Nevin and Williams a hug and started back to Labash's rental car.

As I walked, the man and woman who lived across the street waved to me from their porch.

"Merry Christmas," I hollered. "I told you we'd get that house knocked down."

The man came off the porch and walked toward me, stopping at the fence. "Thank you," he said. "Thank you."

He swept his hands across the calamity of his neighborhood and the half dozen or so other rotting houses.

"But what about the rest of it?"

. . .

I went back to the paper and I sat in my cubicle among the empty pods of cubicles.

Detroit was beginning to wear my ass out. I didn't have the usual reportorial detachment anymore. This was home. This was where I lived. This was where I was raising my kid, and my sister's kid dies in some dark basement not six weeks after I arrive. And this morning I'm watching grown men cheer the demolition of a shit box as though it were the Berlin Wall coming down.

I looked out the window realizing that Detroit was doing something to me that a story's never done to me before. It was hurting.

Ordinarily, a throb of emotion is good for a writer because it feeds his story, it feeds his writing, but then the throb goes away after it's written. But this time it wasn't going away except when I drowned it in wine and then it would return when the wine went away. I felt physically small and cold.

The emotional throb was not informing me so much as eating me. I was tired. And I was beginning to understand now what The Hole really looks like. Before, when I was in the rough places of desperation, I had a plane ticket out. Now I was living in it, a captive, a native son.

TWO

ICE

ICE MAN

INSIDE THE SHELTER, in the rear, near the toilets, two men sat in chairs, shooting dice between their feet. The news played on the wide-screen television set. The TV talk was about money nobody seemed to have anymore. Outside, the arctic wind howled.

The homeless shelter sits in the guts of a skid row ghetto in the city's downtown Cass Corridor. It was packed to the corners, divided with men in one room and women in the other. It smelled like tired bodies.

About one in thirty-five people at any given time in Detroit is without a place to sleep. The problem is so bad and the beds so few that shelters like this one offer only a chair to sit in. The chair is yours as long as you stay in it. Step out for a cigarette and it's a free-for-all. This passes for normal in Detroit. I spent an hour watching the dice game from under a knit hat, occupying a chair that should have gone to someone else who was probably shivering in some crumbling shack that used to function as a home.

I was writing a weather story for the *News*.

The men in front of me were gambling for cigarettes. A die caromed off a chair leg, and the gambler in the parka protested the other man's sloppy dice handling.

"I didn't see the number," he snarled. "You picking up the fucking dice too quick."

"Six!" barked the gambler in the knit pullover, snatching up the cigarette anyhow. A shouting match erupted. Chairs went scattering. Both men were put out in the stinging cold and two men lurking against the wall quickly took their seats.

My cell phone buzzed. It was my brother Frankie calling. He said a friend of his had found a dead body in the elevator shaft of an abandoned building on the south side of the city.

"He's encased in ice, except his legs, which are sticking out like Popsicle sticks," Frankie said.

My brother's friend was one of a strange fraternity in Detroit who call themselves urban explorers. They are a group of grown men who get their thrills traipsing around the ghost buildings, snapping photographs and collecting bits of this and that for odd pieces of art. In other cities, they have tourists.

The explorers had been playing hockey on the frozen waters that had collected in the basement of an abandoned warehouse, my brother explained.

"Why didn't he call the cops?" I asked.

"He said he was trespassing and didn't want to get in trouble."

"Didn't want to get in trouble for trespassing? Really?"

"That's what he says."

Man frozen in ice. Good detail, the reporter in me thought. I arranged to meet my brother to make sure the dead man was true. You never know. It was probably a mannequin. As I was leaving the shelter, I turned for a last look. A man had taken my chair, his feet wrapped in plastic shopping bags.

I got into the raggedy pool car—a Dodge Neon—belonging to the *News'* city desk. I turned the motor over and let the car warm.

Whirr. Whirr. Whirr, the motor whinnied, like a washing machine with bad pulleys.

The dice player in the parka knocked on the window. I rolled it down.

"You a cop?" he asked.

"No."

"Then gimme a dollar."

"That's how you're gonna ask me?"

"Please, gimme a dollar?" he said through a cloud of steam.

I gave him fifty cents, preserving us both some dignity.

I stopped at the *News* office and picked up my partner, Max Ortiz, a photographer. If the dead man was real, then we were going to need a snapshot. We are reporters, after all. We trade in the hard and the obscure. The public is right to despise us, but I knew they couldn't resist the detail of a frozen man either. George Hunter, the Detroit cop reporter with a talent for one-liners, put it this way: "People hate used car salesmen too. But people still buy used cars."

And so Ortiz and I drove to the warehouse in search of an odd-ball dead man.

Whirr. Whirr. Whirr.

The building was known as the Roosevelt Warehouse and once belonged to the Detroit Public Schools as a book and supply repository. The structure burned years before and caused a scandal, since it was filled with thousands of books and balls and crayons and paper and scissors and such—supplies left to rot, despite the fact that Detroit schoolchildren are among the poorest in the country.

This very morning, in fact, a public plea had gone out to the city's parents asking them to send toilet paper with their children to school.

My brother was already at the warehouse with the urban explorer who had, apparently, skated across the body. I was not expecting to see him, since he was worried about those trespassing tickets. He said little to me except that the dead guy was a "fucking trip." He also said, rather unconvincingly, that he had had trouble sleeping since finding the feet a few days earlier and that he wanted me to call the police.

He pointed down at the body. In the middle of the loading dock, there was a gaping elevator shaft. At the bottom of the shaft, you could clearly see a pair of shoes, nothing more. All it appeared I had here was an overimaginative explorer and a pair of discarded discount sneakers. We went down the crumbling steps of the warehouse to get a closer look.

So much rainwater had collected in the basement over the years that we had to stoop down to clear the top of the threshold of the emergency exit, which normally would be eight feet high. We tiptoed across the ice, past a makeshift hockey rink, visible by the light from the barred basement windows, which were now waist high.

The basement was dark and made more eerie by the light diffracting through the support columns of the southern wall. I worried that if we fell through the ice, no one would find us. Preoccupied, I caught my neck on a string of dangling wire and tripped.

"You all right?" my brother asked.

"Shit," I said.

"Over here," said the explorer.

I picked myself up and walked over. There in the cascading light in the central elevator shaft were the shoes, but from this angle there were also shins attached to them. I poked at the shoes with the eraser side of my pencil. I always make notes with pencils in the wintertime. Ball-point pens tend to freeze—same with dogs and people if you leave them outside long enough.

This was no mannequin. This was indeed a man frozen in the ice. His shins had hair. His socks were oddly white, the laces fresh and the sole of the left shoe worn out at the heel. Strangely, the feet were propped up on a pillow that had pooled into the elevator shaft along with other detritus. The hem of a beige jacket could be made out under the ice, as could the contour of his back. The rest of the body looked as though it had vanished.

"Jesus," Ortiz said.

"Yeah," said my brother. "I can't believe he's still got his shoes."

Frankie had brought along his own camera, a digital number with a gigantic lens. Since he had graduated from art school with a degree in photography, my brother was struggling to find a career making pictures. Social documentary, he liked to say.

He snapped a few photographs of the frozen man until he saw Ortiz go to work. Frankie frowned, backed away and deleted his pictures. "Not my shot," he told me later, after the publication of the frozen man story caused an international sensation. "What was I going to do with his picture?" Frankie explained. "Hang it on my wall? Please."

I called a couple homicide cops I know, leaving them messages about the body. I didn't call 911. It didn't seem like it was an emergency.

There was no blood. The man wasn't going anywhere. He would wait. We headed back to the office.

Whirr. Whirr. Whirr.

My cell phone buzzed a few minutes after we arrived at the office. It was one of the cops. "Aw, just give 911 a call," he said. He sounded tired, unconcerned. "We'll be called eventually."

I called 911. A woman answered. I explained it slowly to her.

"Where is this building?" she asked. I pulled up an online map on the photo editor's computer. A crowd of *News* reporters and photographers was gathering around the photo of the frozen man's feet.

"You think it's a story by itself?" I asked one of the paper's more imaginative editors.

"Yes, I do," she said. "It's an important story."

Twenty minutes passed, then 911 called the newsroom. This time it was a man. "Where's this building?"

I explained it again.

He said he'd send a crew out.

Gary Miles, the deputy managing editor of the *News*, told me to hold off writing a story until the body was extricated by the authorities. Maybe we would learn his cause of death and such. So Ortiz and I drove back to the warehouse and waited until sundown. We saw no squad car, no fire truck. We drove home and had a warm supper.

Ortiz and I went back to the warehouse the next morning to check on the frozen man and collect details for the story we would write. Incredibly, he was still there. Now the man became his own story. Two feet in ice, and nobody cared.

A colony of homeless men frequently used the warehouse to keep warm until the nearby shelter along Michigan Avenue opened for the evening and gave out sleeping spaces on the floor by lottery.

One of the men, a bundle of bones and whiskers, was lying under filthy blankets not twenty feet from the shaft.

"You know that guy in the shaft?" I asked him.

"I don't recognize him for his shoes," he said.

"Did you call the cops?"

"No, I figured someone else did," he said. "There's lots of people coming through here with cameras and cell phones."

"He's been down there since last month at least," said his shackmate, who had walked up with some scrap wood to feed the fire in an oil drum.

"I thought it was a dummy myself."

Besides, he said, he'd rather live next to a corpse than play the musical chairs game back at the shelter.

Then he asked: "You got a couple bucks?"

Ortiz took some more photos, this time lighting the scene with a strobe. We drove back to the office and called 911 twice more. Once they hung up. The second time, they answered and took directions. And then they called me back again. This time, I offered to show them where the dead man was.

Ortiz and I drove back out. The firefighters were standing at the wrong building, across the vacant lot. We pointed them toward the elevator shaft across the street.

After a few minutes, one of them emerged. "My God, every time I say I think I've seen it all, I see something like this," said the captain. The firefighters began to extract him with chainsaws.

A police sergeant arrived and called me to his car to make some notes. His city-owned Chevy was smashed on the right front quarter panel. The odometer read 100,000 miles. The floorboards were rotting away, and the sergeant's thin shoes were sitting in a pool of cold water where the gas pedal was. We made small talk. I asked him how business was. "I've got job security, let's put it that way," he said, deadpan.

"Nobody says shit," the sergeant said about murder witnesses. "Now we got to be nice to them. Yeah, like that works. It's a culture of silence and death in this city."

He explained to me how he was trying to get one of his homicide cases reclassified as a suicide, since it may have been possible that a bedridden invalid had plugged himself in the face with a shotgun. "If you look at the blood splatter just right, it is possible," he said hopefully.

"That's one way to close a case," I said, wishing him luck.

The television trucks began to show up, having heard the goings-on over the police scanner. A tall British cameraman could only laugh at the attention the frozen man was now getting. "The people actually alive in this city can't get an ambulance to show up and Mr. Freeze down there has half the fire department helping him. That's the power of the press, mate."

True. The average response time in Detroit for an emergency call to the police is a half hour, give or take; it's little better with ambulances.

It was nearing midnight when the frozen man was finally extracted. He was set on the loading dock to await the meat wagon, the coroner's van.

When it arrived, who should get out but my old pal Mike Thomas, the rapping body collector. I had profiled Thomas a few years earlier for the *Times*—one of those "losers" I wrote about—and he was fired under orders from city hall, since he made the city look bad.

I wrote that he was one of the few people in Detroit who was working. Thomas earned $14 a human corpse and claimed on his tax forms that he had made $14,000—not including the $9 he got paid to collect dead animals that had been mistaken for human beings, which happened more often than one would think.

The difference between a dead dog and a dead man is $5, exactly the amount Henry Ford used to pay for a day's work.

"Hey, Mike!" I yelled. "I thought I got you fired."

"You can't get rid of me, son. I'm like a cock-a-roach."

He appeared to be doing well. He said he had recently moved out of the ghetto, married the mother of his child and cut some new songs. He invited me to his upcoming show, then drove away with the corpse.

The story of the frozen man hit the streets the next morning, the photograph of his feet above the fold and stretching five columns wide. The headline read: FROZEN IN INDIFFERENCE. It was a bold decision by Jon Wolman, the editor and publisher. A dead man with your cornflakes is not the journalistic standard.

The lede read: "This city has not always been a gentle place, but a series of events over the past few, frigid days causes one to wonder how cold the collective heart has grown."

The story was not the only thing that hit the streets that morning. A middle-level manager who had been laid off from General Motors dove out of his downtown high-rise apartment just as a bailiff knocked at the door to evict him.

Also that morning, four thousand winter caps were distributed to the poor by Matty Moroun, the billionaire trucking magnate who owned the Ambassador Bridge connecting Detroit to Canada. As it happened, Moroun also owned the rotting warehouse in which the frozen man was found.

Moroun—Detroit's biggest owner of dilapidated buildings—was giving out the free hats in a public relations move—a sort of "Matty Cares" campaign.

The idea was cooked up by Adolph Mongo, whom Moroun had hired as his Detroit strategist. The free hats and the dead man were pure coincidence, Mongo told me.

I later asked Moroun why he didn't just tear the old book repository down. A gesture like that would do more to soften his image in the newspapers as Detroit's billionaire slumlord than distributing a trailerful of hats. To which he replied: "I'm in the catbird seat here."

Moroun was so rich and the town so broken, no one was going to make him fix shit as long as he had money for lawyers. And he knew it.

The timing of Moroun's hat giveaway stunt was as unfortunate as the selection of hats themselves. They were not your run-of-the-mill knitwear; they were, in fact, ski masks. The type gunmen use to stick up liquor stores.

The picture of the frozen man made its way around the world by way of the Internet, with commentators wondering what in the world was happening in Detroit.

Bailouts, credit-default swaps, international trade blocs. These things were too amorphous, too complex to get your mind around. But a human being left in a crumbling elevator shaft. Everyone could understand that. Had it reached the point of anarchy? a reporter from Barcelona asked me by telephone.

Funny things happen when you run out of money, I told her.

Police officials spent the day trying to explain why it took two days and five phone calls to extricate the man. Some black people complained on the radio talk shows that the *News*—and by extension, I—was racist because it never would have published the picture of a dead white girl from a posh white suburb.

The small, white "art community" in Detroit complained that I was focusing on the negative in a city with so much good. What about all the galleries and museums and music? they complained in a flurry of e-mails and blogs. What about the good things?

It was a fair point. There are plenty of good people in Detroit. Tens of thousands of them. Hundreds of thousands. There are lawyers and doctors and auto executives with nice homes and good jobs and community elders trying to make things better, teachers who spend their own money on the classroom, people who mow lawns out of respect for the dead neighbor, parents who raise their children, ministers who help with funeral expenses.

But these things are not supposed to be news. These things are supposed to be normal. And when normal things become the news, the abnormal becomes the norm. And when that happens, you might as well put a fork in it.

What galleries and museums have to do with a dead man is beyond me. Writing about shit like that in the city we were living in seemed equal to writing about the surf conditions while reporting in the Gaza Strip.

The town turned on me. As if I had committed the outrage of throwing the man down the shaft. The *Free Press* asked why I didn't wait around for the police myself that first night, intimating that I was a sensationalist; that I twisted the facts and sat on a body for a good story.

I got an anonymous phone message from someone claiming to be one of the hockey players. He offered to beat my ass. He said the Showtime network wanted to film the hockey players and their basement scene until I had ruined it with the dead man story. The caller didn't leave a name with his message. A spokesman from Showtime told me he had never heard of urban explorers.

Most odd, I received an e-mail from a man who had also been at the hockey game and claimed he was the first to see the body that morning. He wrote that he took exception to my characterization that his was a cold heart because he stepped around a dead man.

"This discovery presented a moral dilemma to me," he wrote. "Yes, this was a dead human being. However, he had clearly been there for at least 3 months, knowing that the basement had frozen by November. And, as you stated, this building houses many homeless men through the winter. While others may say who-gives-a-shit about the homeless people finding shelter in this warehouse, I wondered if the police would essentially kick all of them out. Maybe one of them would freeze to death?"

He was half right about the homeless people. They were evicted once the police were notified. But no homeless man froze to death as a consequence. They simply moved over to the next abandoned building, an old hotel.

FIRE WOMAN

THE WHOLE FROZEN-MAN episode was dredging up memories I'd tried to bury for a decade. The death of somebody else society considered worthless: my sister.

Nicole died after a night of partying in a bar frequented by prostitutes and heavies called the Flame, located in Brightmoor, on Detroit's west side.

My sister, among her many endeavors in life, was a streetwalker. I wish I could say it wasn't true—but it is. So there you go.

According to the police report, she had climbed into a van with a strange man. He was loaded on liquor and Lord knows what. He was doing eighty miles per hour down a residential street. The street dead-ended at a vacant lot, and beyond the lot was a garage.

My sister was a wild one. And if I remember her right, she probably decided that if she was going to die it wasn't going to be sitting passively in a van while it smashed into a brick wall. She jumped out, straight into a tree.

The van came to a stop, entering the garage through the back. The man inside survived.

At her funeral, the Outlaws motorcycle gang sat in the back of the church, red-eyed, snuffling into their leathers. They had purchased a big horseshoe of roses, the same kind they place around the neck of the winner of the Kentucky Derby. Her name, spelled out in gold lettering, was pinned to it.

NICOLE.

The wake was held in my mother's yard. It was ridiculous. There were bikers and women with the ten-mile stare and proper Catholics and three grown men who wept as they confided to me separately how much they loved my sister and how they were planning to marry her.

I introduced the triplets to one another and watched as they hugged and cried over their shared loss. No hard feelings.

God, I loved my sister. What a hellcat. A fire woman who lived red hot until the flame burned out. Three paramours. A biker gang. A rap sheet and a whole clan weeping over her. I'm proud to have been her brother.

NICOLE.

My mother, predictably, was shattered with guilt and loss. A few weeks after the funeral she asked Frankie and me to take her to Brightmoor so she could lay some flowers at the spot where Nicky died. Then maybe go to the Flame Bar, retrace Nicky's last steps, as though they might offer some sort of explanation as to where it all went wrong.

So we went to the tree in the vacant lot. My mother put her palm upon it and wept. She collected a dry leaf and put it in the pocket of her raccoon coat. Then we went to the Flame.

The place was typical Detroit: cinder block, cheap paneling, a jukebox and a handful of wretches with faces of mud. We sat at the end of the bar, near the door. The mud faces looked at us hard. Lynyrd Skynyrd was playing.

I got a whiskey, my brother got a Southern Comfort and my mother ordered an Amaretto and coffee, except they didn't have coffee here. Or Amaretto. She adjusted her raccoon coat with dignity and smiled.

"Jack Daniel's then. Do you have that? Okay, Jack Daniel's on the rocks. Thank you."

A working girl, gauging by the makeup and cheap spaghetti-strap dress she was wearing in the fangs of winter, approached my mother.

"Do I know you?" barked the hooker, standing with her legs wide apart, her hands on her hips, like there was going to be a fight. My brother stiffened and looked at me with a stony eye. I kept an eye on the leathernecks at the far end of the bar.

My mother looked at the woman with a warm sadness.

"I don't believe so, no."

"Are you lost?"

"No, sweetheart. My daughter used to come here. I wanted to see what it was like."

"Who's your daughter?"

"Her name was Nicole."

"Oh," the girl said, lowering her eyes. "I'm so sorry."

"Thank you," my mother said and sipped her whiskey. "Did you know her?"

"Yes," the girl said, and then went back to the corner and whispered conspiratorially to her people.

We didn't pay for the drinks.

. . .

I've been most everywhere on the planet: war zones, deserts, the Arctic Circle, campaign buses, opium dens, even Albuquerque, but I've never returned to that section of Detroit called Brightmoor. I was afraid of it and would drive miles to avoid it. The memories are too hard.

My mother dealt with the pain a different way. Despite her staunch Catholic beliefs, my mother had my sister cremated. Unable to let Nicky go, not knowing what to do, not wanting to scatter her to the wind, my mother kept her ashes in an urn in her closet, waiting for inspiration. And then the inspiration came.

As I pulled up to the old house on Joy Road, I found my youngest brother, Billy, sitting on a rock in the front yard, crying. He steadied his head in the fold of his elbow, which rested on the stump of an old maple. The tree had died a long time ago from disease.

Traffic out front was unusually light for a workday. When I was a kid, there was always a traffic jam in the late afternoon, around quitting time. But what did I know? I hadn't been home in years.

My brother Frankie told me the Ford plant up the street was down to a single shift.

"Ain't shit left here," he said, frowning at Billy through a menthol.

Billy shuddered, caught a big breath and whimpered again. He was always tender as a boy. When a hatchling fell out of the fir tree near the front door, Billy brought the thing into the house to nurse it. The bird died overnight, and early the next morning I watched from the upstairs window as he gave the thing a private funeral, replete with tears and a cross.

Now he was carrying on like an old Greek widow. I wanted to

kick him in the ribs and tell him to shut the fuck up. He was upsetting the children. Instead, I took the cheap bottle of liquor lying at his knees and poured it in the bushes.

"Stop it," I told him. "She's dead."

My mother sat on the porch, pale and thin, a cigarette burning between her knuckles. Her husband was pacing back and forth shouting, "Goddamn it!"

My stepfather—my *second* stepfather—was old enough to be my grandfather, and he came late in his life to our family. He was from a different time, from that mythological generation of people who worked hard and fought a good war and paid their debts and had respect for the rules. His was a generation that knew nothing about drugs or divorce or moral dissolution. At least that's what he said. He never had any children of his own, but then he married into six—if you count my niece, Ashley, Nicole's daughter, whom he raised since the time she was practically an infant.

And now Ashley was lying in a casket in the funeral parlor next door to our house on Joy Road, dead of a heroin overdose. She died in her other grandparents' basement near the interstate while her father slept nearby.

I looked at the ravaged face of my stepfather and thought to myself that he had finally been baptized in the fires of pain. He was suffering the ultimate feeling of belonging to a family—at least our family.

Stupid kid, she would have grown out of it. Ugly me. Why did I not open my home for her? Had I been away from Joy Road so long that I'd forgotten who I was? The rules and expectations of family? If a brother lies, the other brothers lie to protect him. If a niece calls, her uncle takes her in.

Had I forgotten about the beauty of continuity? My grandmother died in the room where I grew up and my child was now sleeping in that very same room. Had I become that East Coast pretender?

I looked at my wife, who said nothing, except to ask the old people if they needed coffee.

The funeral was held the day before Mother's Day. The cemetery was near a baseball diamond. Children in yellow uniforms were shouting. My mother finally had a place to lay her daughter. In the casket next to her granddaughter. Ashley and Nicole were laid to rest under a red maple.

My brothers and I buried them by shovel. It is a gesture meant for the living, not the dead. It is a promise that we will see each other through until a person's time is no more. It is the last thing we can do for one another. Except pray.

I handed the shovel to my brother Jimmy and looked up at the old people around the grave and considered the great turmoil of human history that they represented. My mother, her ties to the Native people of the Great Lakes and the drifting, whiskered French settlers. My stepfather, whose people emigrated from the port of Danzig, the long-disputed city claimed by both the Germans and Poles, which ignited World War II. My niece's other grandparents, hill folk who hailed from Appalachia and traced their heritage back to the Lowlands of Scotland and the warrior William Wallace.

People from all corners of the earth who came to Detroit to work in its factories and make it one of the most significant cities of history.

I looked up over the grave and surveyed the heaving sobs of my nieces and the strained faces of my brothers. Jimmy looking for work. Frankie on the verge of losing his house. Billy in the screw factory. Somehow, the city of promise had become a scrap yard of dreams. But fighters do what they do best when they've been staggered. They get off their knees and they fight some more.

"How you doing?" I asked Billy over a beer afterward.

"Squeaking by," he answered.

"Sorry I poured your liquor out."

"You owe me four bucks."

JOHNNIE $

THE FROZEN MAN in the elevator shaft was identified a week after being found by the wallet in his back pocket. His name was Johnnie Lewis Redding. DOB 09-29-1952. The medical examiner ruled out murder or drowning since there were no broken bones, no wounds and no water in his lungs.

Most probably, Redding died of a cocaine overdose and was tossed down the elevator shaft by a panicky friend.

It happens all the time with drug addicts. The year before, a man overdosed and his friends stuffed him in a suitcase, threw the suitcase in an SUV, then lit the SUV on fire.

"The way that members of a society die is a reflection of the way society lives," Dr. Carl Schmidt, the Wayne County medical examiner, told me in his office, decorated with Mexican death art. "The point is, there are people like that. And one of the things that separates the human species from all other animals is that we bury our dead. So when we walk away from a dead human being, what does that tell you about the state of things?"

The doctor was right. Like my sister, Johnnie was a human being, worthy of some consideration. I decided to track down his life.

To begin at the end, Johnnie Redding's body had not even been put in its grave before another man moved into his house.

It was a little A-frame wigwam, made of felt and perched on top of an abandoned garage. The wigwam had a framed window and a chimney. It had a river view and a garden. Johnnie had built it with his own hands.

One of Johnnie's street friends whom I had met at the liquor store near the book repository brought me along.

He was beating on the wigwam door, threatening to evict the interloper by force. Even the people of the rough and raw streets have their law.

"You's probably the one who killed Johnnie," Johnnie's friend barked at the plank-board door, alcohol vapors tumbling from his mouth. "You killed Johnnie, and now you sleeping in his bed! You be gone by sundown!"

Johnnie was a second cousin to Otis Redding, the soul singer. His street name was Johnnie Dollar. He was described by people who knew him on the boulevards as a consummate hustler, a pool shark, a block captain who liked a little liquor and a little cocaine. He took handouts and mission food, but he didn't walk around with his hat in his hand, and he didn't get Social Security.

Johnnie, who was fifty-six when he died, painted houses. He hustled pool tables from Ann Arbor to southwest Detroit. When he was low on money, he would sort clothing at the Most Holy Trinity rectory for $10. Sometimes, the church would give him charity bus tickets that he would turn around and sell.

"He didn't have to be out on the streets, but the street life is an adrenaline rush," said the church's homeless director, who had called me after seeing Johnnie's name in my column. "If this was the 1800s, Johnnie would have been a mountain man."

Johnnie came to Most Holy Trinity the first time asking for money to help pay for his pain medication after having all his teeth removed. Johnnie came to Most Holy Trinity the last time asking for money again.

"He wanted bus fare to get out of town," the director remembered. "I wouldn't give it to him. I regret it now."

Johnnie moved around. When he grew weary of the street life, when his body began to shut down, he would go home to relatives to dry out—to get himself right, he liked to say. He stayed with his brother in River Rouge. He had stayed with his sister in Atlanta for six months, then he came back to Detroit and got lost again.

Like a moth to the light, Johnnie gravitated to the corner near the Happy Liquor Store on Fort Street, hanging around with his friends, who called themselves the Bus Stop Boys. Wearing a trench coat and with his pockets bulging, Johnnie passed out $10 bills he'd brought from Georgia and told his friends to buy themselves beer.

"That's why we called him Johnnie Dollar," one of the Bus Stop Boys told me. "He was one of the good ones."

Johnnie Dollar did not have to be on the streets: "It's the only place he could be hisself."

I went to visit Johnnie's brother Homer in River Rouge, a depressed little town downriver from Detroit where young men used to make steel and now make trouble. Homer's house is a neat little Cape Cod left to him by his mother, where both he and Johnnie were raised. According to Homer, his brother was a softhearted man who fell into the street life. Johnnie was one of those men who bounced from odd job to couch to the streets and back. He showed me a picture of his brother from the seventies. Johnnie was lean and dark and wore a wide-brim hat, dark glasses and a white suit with fluted bell-bottoms. He looked like a character from the blaxploitation films of Gordon Parks Jr.—*Super Fly* out on a Friday night, flush with cash from his job at the mill. But the steel mill eventually closed, and Johnnie began partying hard. He ended up on the streets.

"At some point in his life, he didn't want to work anymore," said Homer, a thin, rickety, bald-shaven man. "He got laid off from the steel plant about fifteen years ago, and that was it. But he wasn't homeless. Too many people loved him."

What homelessness is is a matter of opinion. The government has all kinds of ways of counting, and like the unemployed, the government never seems to count them all.

Another of the Bus Stop Boys put it like this: "Homeless means nobody wants you no more. So you can't consider Johnnie homeless."

Except that Johnnie did consider himself homeless. Several months earlier, he had been given a free meal by an outreach group. In exchange for the meal, he had to sign his name, age and address in a manifest. On line no. 7, in shaky block lettering, he wrote: *Johnnie Redding, 56, Homless* [sic]

That didn't mean Johnnie was trash who should have been left at the bottom of an elevator shaft, said Homer as he fought back tears at his kitchen table, rubbing its linoleum as though inspecting it for quality. "I don't know why he said that," Homer croaked. "He was a person. He was a person. He was a person."

Of course he was. Of course Nicky was. And Ashley. And all the other no-name "losers" out there. They all were loved by somebody.

The funeral for Johnnie Redding was held on a windswept Saturday, and nearly three hundred people attended, including some of the Bus Stop Boys. Afterward, as I had a cigarette in the parking lot, an old lady pulled up and asked me if I was the reporter who found Johnnie. Yes, I told her.

"People are fake," she said, referring to the hundreds of Johnnie's Johnnie-come-lately well-wishers. "Put that in your newspaper. People are fake."

Johnnie's funeral was paid for by an insurance policy left on his life by his mother. She suspected something like this might happen. She did not want her children drifting around the earth in death. "She seen too much in life," Homer said.

Johnnie would be buried in the suburb of Westland in a box that was more expensive than anything he owned in life.

The crowd whittled down to about forty people at the cemetery, not including the clergyman. After the prayers and tears, everybody left. Johnnie Redding lay alone and abandoned in his casket. No one stayed to watch him be buried except me and Ortiz and his camera. The soil at the gravesite was rain soaked, and the sides of the earth collapsed as the gravediggers tried to stuff Johnnie in the hole. It would have to be redug, prolonging the burial by a few hours. My feet were cold; wet and cold.

"You got what you need?" I asked Ortiz.

"Yeah."

"Let's get the hell out of here, then. I'm freezing."

We walked off. And Johnnie Redding was left to his lonesome once again.

I went back to the wigwam a couple days later, wanting to tell the new tenant that he was safe now, nobody was coming to take his house. He seemed relieved and invited me to sit down. He bummed a smoke and grew philosophical.

"Nothing's permanent," he said. "We all end up in a box. What do you think this is?"

Then he asked for two dollars for something to eat.

Johnnie, it turned out, had not lived in the wigwam for some time. The new man had claimed it while Johnnie was away in Atlanta. Finders Keepers—that too is an unassailable law of the street.

Understanding this law, Johnnie did not grow belligerent, the man said. Johnnie simply built himself another house of wood and tarpaulin in the culvert below.

His stuff was still in it. A bed. A razor. A pair of reading glasses. A can opener. Near his pillow were two silk neckties and a book: *The Adventures of Tom Sawyer.*

Mama's Boy

With General Motors stock trading at levels not seen since the Great Depression, Kwame Kilpatrick walked out of jail shortly after midnight on February 2, 2009.

Kilpatrick had done ninety-nine days.

By the look of things, incarceration had been good to him. Although his fingernails were in need of their customary manicure, he was twenty-five pounds lighter, and the Afro and shaggy beard he had grown in the Wayne County Hilton made his head and ears appear larger—and so his padded shoulders less ridiculous.

As he emerged through the revolving doors of the concrete jailhouse, he was swallowed in a weird scrum of television cameras and thick-necked Nation of Islam bodyguards who threatened to pulp any reporter who got too close. The police only smirked at the complaining reporters, who did not get too close. I stood far on the fringe.

It was as sad as it was appalling: a black city in which the most prominent leader plundered, pillaged and lied, all the while presenting himself as its guardian angel against the White Devil.

Kilpatrick, who walked into that jailhouse as a quivering-lipped pretender, walked out as the creature he always claimed to be, the preening Hip Hop Mayor. Kilpatrick ducked into an SUV and was chauffeured to the house of his mother, Rep. Carolyn Cheeks Kilpatrick, chairwoman of the Congressional Black Caucus, where she reportedly made him eggs for breakfast.

He probably would have benefited from a few hours spent working in a factory. Factory work tends to give you perspective on the importance of things. Of course in the hip-hop world, work was for suckers.

Not that the automobile executives were much better at running things. Turns out our masters of the universe couldn't manage a grocery store.

Steve Rattner, the Obama car czar, walked into the Renaissance Center, the world headquarters of General Motors located on the Detroit River, and made this assessment:

"Everyone knew Detroit's reputation for insular, slow-moving cultures. Even by that low standard, I was shocked by the stunningly poor management that we found, particularly at GM, where we encountered, among other things, perhaps the weakest finance operation any of us had ever seen in a major company."

The weakest finance operation any of us had ever seen.

Christ, it didn't seem to matter. Black or White. Liberal or Conservative. White collar or Blue. Nobody could run shit. And it wasn't just Detroit. Sacramento, Washington, D.C., Wall Street. The entire country was being run into the ground by a generation infected with incompetence and greed.

Consider that Rattner himself was being sued by the attorney general of New York and investigated by the Securities and Exchange Commission for his involvement in a kickback scheme involving the state's pension fund and his investment firm.

Corruption and ineptitude were a national sickness and they were killing us. But Detroit, it cannot be denied, had a certain *flair*.

Pain Never Feels Good

AFTER A FULL morning of having his balls busted at the screw factory for eight stinking bucks an hour, Billy walked out. Bruce Springsteen–style, with his fist in the air. The guys who once hated him shouted, "Much respect, man!"

It was the best day of work he ever put in there.

My brothers and I and our cousin Johnny got together in Billy's basement to do some drinking. He was renting a small two-bedroom Cape Cod about a quarter mile down the road from the house the sheriff locked him out of, the one he wrote the mortgage note on, the one not too far from the interstate.

We drank well into the morning. Our brother Jimmy passed out with his head on the table and Frankie snored like a tractor on a threadbare couch. Johnny asked Billy if he wanted to come to *his* factory, where Johnny worked as a foreman. Johnny told Billy he could probably get him $10.50 an hour plus overtime. And if Billy showed up and did the job with no absenteeism, then after ninety days he could probably get Billy on full time with higher wage and bennies.

My brother jutted his square, inebriated chin into the air. He pointed a finger. He moved to say something. And when he opened his mouth, the dental bridge fell out and bounced into the ashtray. Billy looked down quizzically, then plucked it from the ashes, blew on it and popped it back into place.

Billy got around to answering my cousin's offer with this: "No way."

"Suit yourself," Johnny said with a shrug. "Jobs are awful hard things to sneeze at."

Billy just shrugged.

"What the fuck?" I shouted. "It's a better chance. Look at your fucking teeth!"

"I still got dreams," Billy said after some drunken silence. "If I take that job I'm just admitting that I gave up."

"Gave up? You've got a family."

"I've got dreams, Char," he croaked. "And a factory just isn't part of it. I've got more in me."

When the bank began moving in on Frankie's house, Frankie didn't want to make a deal. He wanted out. The place was worthless, what with the hookers and rats flooding into the neighborhood. What was the sense of trying to dig your way out of a hole by putting the dirt in your pockets? Frankie went looking for boxes to pack up his home.

Boxes are expensive—about four and a half bucks for the big ones. But Frankie found a guy selling them cheap up on 20 Mile

Road. A buck apiece. When Frankie got there, he saw the stamp on the side: MADE IN CHINA.

"Motherfucker, don't we make anything anymore?"

"Not so's you could afford it," the guy said.

Frankie bought two loads of the Chinese boxes and we went to pack his house. We loaded the moving truck in the rain. I took the metal gates as a memento.

Frankie and his family moved to a nice three-bedroom house in a working-class suburb a few miles down the road. The place had a main street and ice cream parlors and children actually played in their front yards. It was the first time in his adult life that my brother did not own his home.

"Maybe it was for the best," I said, drinking a bottle of beer and scanning the quiet street. "This is a really nice neighborhood. It's got to feel good."

Frankie looked at me with a crooked eye. "Char. Despite what they say in the poetry books, pain never feels good."

SCREEN DOORS

I RECEIVED A letter. It was typewritten with no return address and unsigned. It was from an anonymous neighbor complaining about a teacup-size wind chime I had hung on my porch. The anonymous neighbor wrote that now that the weather was warm and people had their windows open, the little bell was distracting and my cooperation in removing it would be greatly appreciated.

It would have been a funny little note had it not been so outrageous. For one, a freeway runs directly behind my house. Before I made an ass of myself and started banging on doors demanding that the anonymous note writer step forward, I decided to take a cooldown drive.

I cruised through Detroit trying to get lost in the sunshine and the radio. Then I spotted a tumultuous cloud of black smoke and drove for it like it was the lodestar.

The smoke came from a tumbledown ghetto neighborhood where a white vinyl house was burning savagely, kicking up the acrid plume. A horde of neighborhood people were blocking the street so the firefighters couldn't gain entrance with their trucks. The engine driver was leaning on his horn, which reminded me of the wailing cries of animals at a slaughterhouse. I thought of my little wind chime.

A mini-riot was about to erupt, with the firemen screaming at a man who had blocked the street with his van. I jumped out of my car and ran toward the crowd.

"What's going on?" I asked a heavyset woman with her hair in a cloth, showing her my press card.

"That be a crack house," she said. "We been calling the police every day, but nobody does nothing. That house be wild and we got children living here. So somebody lit the house on fire and nobody on this block wants it put out."

I told this to the battalion chief, who finally managed to negotiate his rigs through the crowd without incident.

"I can't say I blame them," he said. "Sometimes people gotta do for themselves."

Strange things had been happening in the fire department. One of the men who worked alongside Walt Harris on the morning of his death was sent to work at Ladder Co. 14, also on the east side of the city.

The guy took the death of Harris especially hard. He had turned to the Bible and was studying to become an ordained minister.

He was reading by lamplight on an early Tuesday morning just after midnight and attempted to create a little mood by lighting some incense and dousing the harsh light of a floor lamp by placing a towel over it.

Then the ladder company received a call for a fire at an abandoned apartment complex.

The sleepy-eyed firefighter jumped into his bunker gear, forgetting to take the towel off the lamp.

It seems that nobody in the crumbling neighborhood saw the flames cascading from the firehouse or cared enough to call it in, even though fire was leaping out high above the window frames. In fact, the fire was discovered by the firefighters themselves as they returned from their call.

Laughably, they could not put out the blaze because they had no engine to pump water from the fire hydrant. As it happens, the city decommissioned the engine at the firehouse in a cost-cutting measure.

Inspectors came to talk. I eavesdropped on the whole conversation because another guy had called me with a cell phone in his pocket. The Bible-reading firefighter was scared. As much as he probably wanted to leave Detroit, he needed this job.

"Man, I'm telling you, I didn't have nothing to do with it," he shrieked.

Crestfallen, he disappeared for the better part of a day, which launched a manhunt of firefighters concerned that he would take his own life.

In the end, the investigation ruled it an electrical fire and not another word was spoken about it.

Unbelievably, the same thing—nothing—was being done with the investigation into Walt Harris's death. It was a murder because it happened during an arson—someone had torched the house with a can of gasoline.

In New York or Los Angeles, there would have been an elite homicide squad investigating the death of a man in uniform. But here in Detroit, no manhunt had been launched. No task force assembled. The Harris case had been given over to a single overworked homicide detective, and so it sat on the back burner growing stale.

People in uniform will tell you that no one life is more important than another. The lives of a white cop, a black fireman, a minister and a drug addict all have equal value. But the presumption is that if a person in uniform is killed with impunity, if such a killer is allowed to run free, then no regular citizen is safe. So for the sake of civil order, when a person in uniform is murdered, heads must get knocked, doors must be kicked in and every available cop is put to the task.

In Harris's case, the sole detective's name was Tony Wright. I knew him well. He had been the partner of Mike Carlisle, and I had tailed the two of them a few years earlier when they were hunting down a serial killer. Wright was a good cop, overworked and waiting to retire. I called him from home.

"Tony, what the fuck is going on with Walt's case?"

"It's just me," Wright said. "I'm frustrated. I'd like to solve this case. But I've picked up two more cases since this one. Then I've got to be in court tomorrow. It just goes on and on and on."

I called James Tate, the police department mouthpiece. Poor schmuck. He had to make the department's shit smell decent. He had to tap-dance around the Kilpatrick scandal. He accomplished this by never giving a straight answer.

"We've got a few leads on this case," Tate said, "but if people aren't talking, they aren't talking."

"James, you've only got one guy working this case," I said.

"You've got to remember that we've got three hundred twenty-five other homicide cases out there."

"But this is a guy in uniform."

"It is what it is," Tate said. "I'm just the talking head here."

The situation had grown so ridiculous that the firefighters themselves were going door to door trying to develop leads. But the only thing a fireman is going to accomplish by stepping into the middle of a murder investigation is to fuck it up.

So I wrote the story: HERO GOES FORGOTTEN.

Almost immediately, my boss, Miles, got a call from a deputy chief of police and a junior officer from the homicide squad. They were not pleased with the piece and complained that Wright had not said those things to me. They said I had made them up out of thin air.

Miles said he would have to hear it directly from Wright.

As it happened, Wright was in the room with his commanding officers. They put him up to the speaker phone.

I made a mistake by putting Wright's name in the paper. His balls were in a sling and I placed them there. I imagined him book-ended by the brass, scowling, like he was the suspect of an interrogation. You'd think a grown man would know better. I couldn't blame the detective for whatever he was about to say.

"Go on, Wright, tell him," the deputy chief growled.

"I know Charlie," Wright told my boss. "He's a good dude. I talked to him the other night and I know he was meaning to do the right thing. I'll leave it at that."

Wright could have thrown me under the bus. He didn't because that's how real men behave. Now because he acted like a man, he'd probably be walking the beat in some hellhole on the far northwest side.

There are still a lot of good people in this city trying to hold it together with gum and bailing wire. And I believe Wright wanted me to get done what he could not. Newspapers and journalism still mattered to the community in some way. The work could be important for those without a voice. It could help. That's what Wright was saying by saying almost nothing at all.

In the meantime, Harris's partner Mike Nevin was promoted to lieutenant and transferred from Squad 3 to Engine Co. 38, a firehouse located on the tinder-trap east side.

He and his men were out checking fire hydrants on a spring morning when one of the deckies—fire department speak for grunts—found a screen door torn off its hinges at an abandoned house. The deckie threw the door on the back of the rig and the engine drove off, with Nevin in command. It seemed like no big deal. The copper piping in the old house had been scavenged, the meter box, the electrical wiring, even the garage door. Inside the garage was a pile of trash and human excrement. Who would miss the screen door?

Their firehouse didn't have a screen door and the flies were getting in. Detroit firefighters have been repairing their firehouses like this for decades. Toilets, doors, lumber, bricks. The city never cared. No one ever complained. And it was cheaper than paying for upkeep.

This time, however, a neighbor caught Nevin and his crew on tape. The neighbor sent the tape to a local news station. The news station put its crack reporter on the job. Within days, Nevin and his men were fired for "looting" the city.

Nevin was beside himself. Maybe he should have told the deckie to leave the door be. Maybe he shouldn't have revealed to investigators that Walt Harris's alarm didn't trigger when the roof collapsed on him. Maybe he shouldn't have called the city leadership an abject and complete failure in my newspaper column. Maybe he shouldn't have told Rep. Sander Levin to kiss his balls. There was a lot Nevin probably shouldn't have done. The brass hated him, and the brass had his balls now.

The irony is, Nevin used to have a little screen door business. He knew the thing wasn't worth twenty bucks.

I went to Nevin's disciplinary hearing, a meeting open by law to the public. I waited in the foyer of fire headquarters downtown, making notes in my book. There was a glass case containing the photographs of the department's fifteen ranking executives—all were black and all appointed. The department in total is about half black and half white, and an all-black command staff would be grounds for a discrimination lawsuit in most other cities. But this is metropolitan Detroit. Race is a way of life.

A man in uniform approached me. I recognized him from the glass case: Second Deputy Commissioner James W. Mack Jr.

"May I ask what you are doing here?"

"I'm a reporter covering Lieutenant Nevin's disciplinary hearing."

"I know who you are and I'm going to have to ask you to leave," he said, taking me by the elbow and leading me to the elevators. He smiled like a lizard.

I wrote his name in my tablet.

It was quiet in the elevator. He watched the lighted numbers change. I watched him watch the lighted numbers change. I never took my eyes off him. I was staring directly at the man. Mayors come and go, but it is the footmen who tie the knots and divide the bag. The longtime little men. Bureaucrats. Cockroaches.

The elevator reached the ground floor.

"Here you are."

"Sir," I said, "the only reason you have Nevin up there on charges is because he spoke to me and he told the truth. So I promise you one thing. I'm going to go through all the paperwork, all the contracts, and I'm going to find it."

"What do you suppose you'll find?" he asked with a face.

"The money," I said. "I'm going to find out who ruined this department. I'm going to find those screen doors."

"Good luck with that, sir, and have a nice day."

I stepped outside into the doom and the gloom of the Michigan spring and watched steam hiss from the sewer caps. All of downtown Detroit is powered and heated by steam produced from a massive waste incinerator located on the edge of a neighborhood. The whole goddamned downtown running on garbage. A whole neighborhood full of kids choking on the smoke of burning diapers and car batteries.

I stood under the granite cornices of the fire headquarters where a covey of pigeons was huddled against the rain. I roasted up a Winston and thought about things.

It was funny to me at first: the corruption and incompetence and selfishness. But now I was looking at it in a different way: the leadership was ruining people. Or worse, killing them.

Kilpatrick had been taken out. So too had Monica Conyers. But he was only the head of the snake. And she was a dipshit. I couldn't laugh at it anymore. I was part of it, related to it, stuck in it. I was home and I wasn't leaving. I couldn't.

I decided I was going to keep that promise. I was going to find out who was responsible for the outrage of murderers walking free while the city burned night after night. I was going to become a real reporter. Someone had to answer for this shit. The dignified burial of Johnnie Dollar and the demolition of Harris's death house gave me confidence. The people of Greater Detroit deserved better than to be robbed by their leaders and forgotten by their neighbors.

I threw my cigarette butt into the sewer grate. I looked up into the rain. That's when a bird shit on my face.

THE FIFTH

DRINKING WAS THE only thing that would make Detroit go away. My life was populated with dead men and liars and desperate people who would call me at all hours of the evening, and the only door of escape I could find was at the bottom of a bottle.

One evening my wife and I dropped our daughter off at her grandmother's and we got good and loaded on red wine. Then the phone rang. It was a cop buddy of mine with another piece of nasty news. Three men dead on a lawn and nobody had bothered to call the authorities for four hours.

Entranced, I ignored my wife. A mistake. When I hung up the phone, she was eating a piece of cold pizza.

"I'm getting sick of this."

Apparently she was fed up with the stories of murder victims lit on fire in abandoned houses and women who found their boyfriends hanging dead from a pair of pantyhose while dressed in their lingerie.

"Fucking deal with it," I said. "It's putting pizza in your fat mouth."

"Fuck you," she hissed.

"Fuck me?" I jumped out of my chair, took her by the wrist and smeared the pizza in her face. She slapped me.

"I'm calling 911, you fucking asshole."

"Go ahead. I'm going to bed."

I was upstairs sleeping, nude except for a pair of striped underpants—my own—when the cop knocked on our door.

"Charlie," my wife yelled. "The police are here."

She had called 911 and then, like a spoiled sorority girl, hung up the phone. Apparently no one informed my wife that the cops come anyway in the suburbs. I poured myself down the stairs in nothing but those electric striped underpants. I was surprised to see the cop—not on the porch but standing in my living room, the blue lights from his cruiser lighting up the neighborhood.

He had tricked my wife into letting him in.

"Yes, Officer?"

He was a short, stout guy with a round, slightly oily face like a ham hock sealed in plastic.

"Put some clothes on," he ordered.

I tried some drunken legalese. "Is there justifiable reason why you have entered my domicile, Officer? Do you have reason to believe there is imminent danger here? Have I made a furtive motion?"

He shined a light on my wife. "She has blood on her face."

I don't know where the bitterness comes from, but when provoked, I spew like a warm can of beer. It causes problems.

"It's pizza sauce," I sneered. "Taste it."

"Put your hands in front of you," ordered Officer Ham.

I did as he said. He slapped handcuffs on me.

"Go upstairs and get him some clothes," he told my wife.

"Do no such thing," I ordered her.

"You don't want clothes?" he said with an arch of the eyebrow.

"Officer, I wish to invoke my Fifth Amendment right to remain silent so as not to incriminate myself."

"Just put some fucking clothes on."

"Officer, I wish to invoke my Fifth Amendment right to remain silent so as not to incriminate myself."

"Suit yourself."

The cop led me by my shoulder across the lawn into the back of the squad car. I could see a neighbor peering out the window at the spectacle of the wife-beating redneck with the feral alley cat and church-bell wind chime being led to the pokey, barefoot and in striped blue underpants.

I woke up in the morning in a jail cell, shivering in my striped underpants. There was no one else in the cell except a cockroach tending to a half-eaten egg sandwich lying near the stainless-steel toilet.

I felt bad, hollow. A middle-aged fuckup crumbling under the bulk of a dying city. It had infected my private life, which was no longer separate from my public one. People took photos and said shitty things about me that were mostly true, but the annoying thing was they were only guessing. And now I probably had two court dates: one with the criminal judge, one with the divorce judge. I thought about my little girl and wondered what I had done bringing her back to this shit hole.

I tried to place a collect call to Frankie on the jailhouse telephone. It was one of the few numbers I had committed to memory. But the jailhouse phone was malfunctioning, the wires crossed or something. I could hear the woman's conversation in the next cell.

"Tell him when I see him again I'm gonna put a knife in his neck," the woman was telling her son. "Tell that motherfucker I'll finish the job, soon's I get outta here."

I laughed. It was like a bucket of fresh water for my spirit. No matter how bad I had it, I wasn't that crazy bitch in the next cell plotting to finish her boyfriend off with picnic cutlery or the sharp end of a No. 2 pencil.

"Hey," I shouted, knocking on the one-way glass above the wooden bunk. "I want my phone call."

"Stop beating on the glass, asshole," came the response through the intercom. "They know you're here."

"I want some shoes," I shouted back. "I'm cold."

"There's a pair outside the door, asshole."

"I want a Koran," I shouted one more time. "It's my constitutional right. I want a Koran."

"Put a cork in it, asshole," said the voice in the box. He may not have had an extensive vocabulary, but he was consistent if nothing else. I suppose that's what you want in your peace officers.

And he was right. I was acting like an asshole because deep inside that chasm I could hear my own echo: You *are* an asshole.

The cell door opened about twenty minutes later and there sitting near the threshold was a stack of clothes and a pair of sneakers. "Put those on," said the sergeant. He was different from the guy who'd arrested me.

"Your wife refuses to file an official complaint, so you get to go."

"I appreciate it," I said.

"Don't thank me, thank her," he said. "Look, we got a lotta guys like you coming through here lately. You know what I'm saying? Things are hard. People have a few pops to wash it away. Things get out of hand. All of a sudden we got you here. That sound about right?"

"Yes sir, it does," I said, breaking my Fifth Amendment boycott, pulling up my trousers.

"Let me give you some advice," he said. "The next time it starts up, pick yourself a place in the house and go there. You understand? 'Cause we got your name in the computer now."

"Thanks, Sergeant," I said, really meaning it.

I stepped out into the Sunday morning light, hungover and ashamed. I wondered if I was going to make the Sunday papers.

I wasn't sure where I was. I was in another town, picked up by a neighboring police force, another jurisdiction. My wife was idling in the parking lot looking sad. I waited for an emotion before deciding what to do. Finding it, I walked to the car and she rolled down the window.

"How's the baby?"

"She's at my mom's. She's fine. I'm sorry."

"Not more than me," I said.

I kissed her and told her I'd walk the miles home. Instead, I walked to Frankie's rented house nearby. People mowed their yards here. You could hear the wind and birds. When I got to Frankie's house, his girls were playing in the front yard, unattended. I had never seen that in his old neighborhood. Maybe things were turning around for him.

As for me, I didn't know who I was fighting anymore. Probably myself, and I was killing him. I lay down in Frankie's backyard in the tall grass under the catalpa trees and fell asleep.

THREE

FROM THE ASHES

Boom

DETROIT WOULD NEVER have been if not for the beaver.

Louis XIII, the ambiguously homosexual king of France, who had a double set of teeth and a pronounced stutter, was fond of prancing about the streets of Paris wearing a beaver-pelt hat.

As it is with Europeans, the king of England decided he too enjoyed prancing about the streets of London in a beaver-pelt hat. The style caught on and the beaver became all but extinct in Europe.

The next king of France, Louis's son Louis XIV, dispatched men to the New World to procure more beaver skins and instructed a man who called himself the "sieur de Cadillac" to establish a fort in the lower Great Lakes to block the English advance on his fur monopoly.

On June 5, 1701, Cadillac and two hundred men shoved off from Montreal in twenty-five canoes. Commandant Cadillac was a hustler. His real name was Antoine Laumet, and it is believed he had stowed away on a ship to escape debts in France, arriving in the New World in 1683.

He quickly learned the land and the customs of the natives, which made him invaluable to the crown. Cadillac also illegally trafficked in liquor and furs with the natives and was for a short time thrown in prison. That would also make Cadillac Detroit's first dope dealer.

Cadillac chose the strait—*détroit* in French—that connects Lake Erie to Lake Huron, the gateway to the entire Great Lakes basin and its copious beaver, as the site of his new Fort Pontchartrain du Détroit.

And thus Detroit was born in July 1701.

My family was here from the earliest days. It began with my ancestor Joseph Chevalier, a Frenchman from Normandy who came to Montreal to carve a life out of the wilderness. He took as his wife Françoise-Marthe Barton, one of the *filles du roi*, or king's daughters, a group of eight hundred women sent under the sponsorship of Louis XIV to marry French settlers and populate New France.

She gave Joseph Chevalier thirteen children including Jean Chevalier, a *coureur de bois*, literally a runner of the woods—a wild breed of man who lived among the natives, drank and smoked heavily, could paddle a canoe at fifty-five strokes a minute and thumbed his nose at the authority of the crown.

Chevalier arrived at Fort Detroit in 1705, not four years after its founding by Antoine Cadillac.

Detroit was a dangerous frontier town with three bands of rival Indians living on its outskirts. In 1706, a priest and a soldier were killed in an Indian uprising, making my great-grandfather Chevalier a material witness to the first recorded murder in Detroit. And like tens of thousands of murders in Detroit since then, the priest's homicide remains unsolved. A cold case.

.   .   .

Detroit in the nineteenth century was the center of the nation's carriage and wheel and stove industries because of its lumber and the rich ore deposits in the upper reaches of Michigan. This set the stage for tinkerers like Ransom Olds, who was among the nation's largest carriage manufacturers before he turned to cars. Henry Ford, a farmer, built his first automobile plant in Highland Park in 1899. Detroit would rapidly become the world's machine shop, its factory floor, growing in population from 300,000 to 1.3 million in the twenty-five years following Ford's grand opening.

General Motors was founded in 1909, and a host of other car companies blossomed: Chrysler, Packard, Studebaker, Hudson, Olds, and Dodge among them.

In 1919, the young and hungry men of GM devised an ingenious scheme to supplant Ford as the number-one carmaker in the world.

Credit.

Ford, a notorious miser and social ascetic, did not believe it was a good idea for Americans to buy consumer goods like automobiles on credit. He opted for the layaway plan, allowing a buyer to pay a little each month until he had the car paid for in its entirety. The problem is this took five years, and it was hard to hold on to a factory job for that long.

So General Motors came up with a financing arm: the General Motors Acceptance Corporation, or GMAC.

Over the next decade, most durable goods like cars and refrigerators and washing machines were bought on a down payment and a monthly installment payment plus interest. The first credit card was issued in 1950 by the Diners Club, and by that time General Motors had overtaken Ford as the number-one carmaker in the world. American dominance as well as consumerism and debt were in full bloom.

Nearly a century after its founding, GM had more than $1 trillion loaned to car buyers and had expanded into other businesses like home mortgages.

During the Roaring Twenties, fueled by growing assembly lines, the population of the Motor City surpassed those of Philadelphia, Boston and Baltimore, old East Coast port cities that were founded on maritime shipping when the world moved by boat.

The Europeans marveled at the rapturous whirl of making and spending in the new America. At the center of this economic dynamo was Detroit and its flaming smokestacks.

"It is the home of mass production, very high wages and colossal profits, of reckless installment buying and shifting labour surplus," wrote the British politician and author Ramsay Muir in 1925. "It regards itself as the temple of a new gospel of progress to which I will venture to give the name Detroitism."

The air over Detroit was ashen and sooty, the color of a filthy dishrag. The water in the river was so poisoned, it was said you could bottle it and sell it as paint thinner. Detroit was choking on industry.

In 1934, the last beaver was sighted in the Detroit River.

BUST

On June 1, 2009, General Motors declared bankruptcy, following Chrysler, which had done so a month earlier. Ford was teetering.

For the first time in anyone's memory, every auto factory in Michigan sat idle. Plans were made to reconstitute the companies, phase out models and close dealerships. More than 300,000 people in Michigan lost their jobs. In a town founded by a man named Cadillac, you could no longer purchase a Cadillac.

It was a historic day and I took a swing by the Renaissance Center downtown, GM's headquarters. Japanese and German media crews were camped across the street, waiting to beam live to Tokyo and Berlin the news that they had finally won.

I gave a German the "welcome to town" thumbs-up and he gave me a self-important frown. Funny, foreign journalists are even bigger assholes than their American counterparts.

Regardless of their national origin, most of the media knew nothing about the machinations in the boardroom, but that never stopped them from pretending they did.

If the German had bothered to ask I would have told him the Renaissance complex was half empty and the executive suites faced Canada, so the GM executives wouldn't have to look down on the devastation of Detroit.

Sniffing for a story, I jumped in my '73 Checker cab—made in Kalamazoo, Michigan—and headed for Hamtramck, remembering the American Axle plant located there.

The plant, which straddles Detroit and Hamtramck, was the largest in Axle's sprawling worldwide manufacturing complex. It mainly produced axles for GM's heavy-duty pickups, which accounted for about three quarters of its sales.

Beleaguered Hamtramck, an industrial hamlet of 22,000 people that is completely surrounded by the city of Detroit, was increasingly becoming a town with too many mice and not enough men. A welfare office opened on Joseph Campau Street, an almost unthinkable concept in this once Polish, once working-class town.

The mayor had her car stolen, and an elderly city councilman tried to beat off a carjacker with a cane. He failed, and the carjacker made off with his jalopy. And his cane.

Since American Axle was spun off from General Motors and reconstituted in 1994, the UAW negotiated with American Axle, not General Motors.

When I had arrived back home the previous winter, Local 235 here was on strike. It was a cold, bitter dispute, complete with old-school fires in the oil drums. The unionized workers, numbering nearly two thousand at the time, lost. They gave in to deep wage cuts, in some cases from $28 an hour to $14, in exchange for keeping their jobs. Apparently it was not enough.

In contrast, Dick Dauch, the CEO and chairman of American Axle, was given an $8.5 million bonus by his board of directors after the strike and gave assurances to the workers and the city of Hamtramck that he would keep production there. It was lip service.

At six A.M., with the streets of Hamtramck all but empty, Bill Alford, the president of Local 235, shambled up the street to punch in for work at Plant No. 8. He cut a pathetic figure, one shoe untied and dressed in a hockey sweater with a large *C* embossed on the chest. *C* is for captain, but Alford was now the captain of almost nobody.

As GM planned to officially declare bankruptcy, more than five hundred workers employed at the plant quietly received a letter by FedEx informing them that they had been indefinitely laid off.

Normally, presidents of local unions do not go to work at the plant, as management prefers not to have labor agitators on its factory floors. But when there were too few employees to do the work, Alford was required by contract to return to the plant.

And so Alford was left with the humiliating task of having to pack up his workplace and load crates of tools and machinery onto a truck bound for Texas and Mexico.

"They don't want a middle class," Alford told me as we stood in the rain outside the plant, his shoestring still untied. "I see that in the future people will have to move to Mexico for a job. This is a dark day for the American laborer."

I went to see about an interview with Dick Dauch at his corporate headquarters down the street. I was thrown off the property by security.

I went back to the union hall, where workers were flowing in trying to find out what the hell was going on with their jobs.

"I'm not ever going to buy another Chevy," said a hard, lean man named Jeff Johnson. Johnson received the layoff notice on Saturday, his birthday, mistaking the FedEx package for a present.

"I'm not buying another new car because I'm not ever going to be able to afford a new car."

Johnson laughed. "It's a good thing they ain't letting us back in there. I'd fuck up all that machinery that I could, motherfuckers." And with that he was gone.

Dauch had betrayed Hamtramck and I wrote the story that way. Nevertheless, my paper was the voice of the business class and our executives belonged to the same social clubs as our masters of the universe. One of them stopped at my desk to explain to me Dauch's thinking and his unhappiness with my story.

"Look," he said to me, taking a chair next to my desk. He was wearing a starched blue shirt and suspenders. "Dick believed in the competitiveness of U.S. manufacturing and he tried to make it work. But he couldn't, not with the absenteeism and the entitlement mind-set of the Michigan worker."

Apparently one third of Axle's workforce was out sick on any given day of the week, he explained.

"How do you know that?" I asked. "You just going to take his word for it, or does he have paperwork to back it up? Tell Dick for me, I'll meet with him any time of the day, but if he's going to make claims like that, I need to see the proof."

"Okay, Charlie," he said, patting me on the shoulder. "Try to be a little more discerning in your assessments."

Upset, I went outside for a cigarette. The city, what's left of it, burns night after night. Nature—in the form of pheasants, hawks, foxes, coyotes and wild dogs—had stepped in to fill the vacuum, reclaiming a little more of the landscape each day. The streets were empty and cratered. The skyscrapers were holograms. I stood and admired a cottonwood sapling growing out of the roof of the Lafay-ette Building. This was like living in Pompeii, except the people weren't covered in ash. We were alive.

By the end of the year, with Hamtramck on the verge of bank-ruptcy and an official unemployment rate near 15 percent in the state of Michigan, the price of stock in American Axle had tripled. Dauch got a $1 million raise.

And if you needed a metaphor for how retrograde things were becoming, a beaver was sighted nesting in the Detroit River for the first time in seventy-five years.

Two Plus Two Equals Three

DETROIT GOT A new leading man that spring. Dave Bing was elected Detroit's third mayor in eight months with an underwhelming voter turnout of 14 percent.

Bing first came to Detroit as the number-two pick in the NBA draft in 1966 and played nine seasons for the Pistons, ending up in the Hall of Fame. After retiring from basketball, he started his own business manufacturing auto parts in Detroit. He ran his mayoral campaign touting this executive acumen.

An elegant, introverted and geriatric figure, Bing neglected to tell voters that his business was failing and that it had existed hand-to-mouth for a number of years. With the collapse of the auto industry, GM and Ford told Bing they couldn't float his company anymore, even if it meant cutting strings with one of the few minority contractors out there.

Bing also failed to mention that his campaign manager had served two years in federal prison for a crime involving a sludge-hauling contract with the water department under Coleman Young.

Nor did he mention that one of his legal advisers had been indicted on charges that he acted as consigliere for the Highwaymen motor-cycle gang.

But after the nightmare of Kilpatrick, Detroiters wanted calm. And Grandpa Bing was just the warm glass of milk they were look-ing for. From the outset, Bing's strategy was not so much to root out bad apples as to keep the apple cart from tipping over.

His first major announcement was that he had decided to keep James Barren, the chief of police, despite the fact that murder was spiraling out of control. Bing also promoted James Mack—who had bounced me from Mike Nevin's disciplinary hearing—to executive commissioner of the fire department, despite the fact that heart attack victims were dying in snowdrifts waiting for an ambulance that never seemed to arrive.

In the blink of an eye, Bing had changed nothing.

Chief Barren got to work quickly. And he was a genius. Without so much as pulling a gun or reorganizing the bone-brittle depart-ment, he managed to make the murder rate fall at a world-record pace.

His department claimed that homicides had declined 25 percent over the past year, while he was in charge, of course.

It was a drop of historic proportions, so huge that the city should have thrown a parade, complete with clown carts and lemonade tanks and banners that read: DETROIT! AT LEAST WE'RE NOT BALTIMORE!

But oddly, the announcement was greeted with a midnight silence. It didn't even rank as a front-page story.

Still, some people read it. Homicide cops read it, and a couple of them called me out to lunch to tell me that the brass was cooking the books. There was no feasible scenario, short of criminal conduct, they surmised, in which the murder count could be that low.

We met at some dark dump near the ballpark where the Tigers play.

"Check out the numbers, there's no way," said Sgt. Mike Martel, a large man who seemed to wear his attitude in his mustache. It was thick and bristled and twitched with hassle. "If they make it look better than it is, then we don't get the money we need to keep a lid on this shit hole. You know what kind of crap we're driving around in? You know how many cases we've got to handle?"

I said I did, remembering the pool of water in the foot well of the car driven by the detective in charge of the case of Johnnie Dollar, the frozen man.

The other detective wore a mustache too. He was shorter than Martel. And meaner. He had a gray smile. He told me about the time a homicide detective had to take a bus to a crime scene because there were no working pool cars in the squad.

"They're robbing the city fucking blind, Charlie," he said, rubbing his fingers together. "In this city two plus two equals three."

"Kilpatrick. Bing. Whatever. Nothing's fucking changed," growled Martel, squeezing the life out of his lemonade glass. He looked over his shoulder, on the lookout for anybody from the homicide squad who might rat him out for talking to a reporter. Seeing nobody, he drank the glass whole.

I went to visit Dr. Schmidt, the medical examiner. Every murder victim has to funnel through the morgue, and so I knew I could get a true and accurate count there.

I was shown to the examination room. The cooler was stacked

to the ceiling with cadavers in vinyl zip body bags, and a tractor-trailer refrigerator truck in the parking lot handled the overflow. It reeked of spoiled cherries. The floors were sticky.

"What's that all about?" I asked Dr. Schmidt, the poetical man of death, as he came into the room with a quick shuffling step, his hand extended.

"That is a sign of how bad things have gotten," he said matter-of-factly. "It's the economy. Some people really have to make a choice of putting food on the table or burying their loved ones. It is very sad, really. In all of my years here, I have never seen it this bad."

The people of Wayne County now couldn't afford to bury their loved ones. More than 250 sat unclaimed. The doctor pointed out the saddest case—the cadaver of an elderly man that had been here for two years, shuffled to the bottom of the pile as his kinfolk waited for a ship to come in.

"You might say this is a fairly decent barometer of where we are as a society," the good doctor said with a shrug.

Poor Grandpa. I put it in my notebook. His predicament wasn't good news, but it smelled like front-page news.

And then the doctor handed me a spreadsheet with more front-page news than I was looking for—nearly four hundred people had been murdered in Detroit in 2008—not three hundred, as was claimed by the city.

The police were right. The police were lying.

I was fishing up in the lake country when I got the phone call. The police high command on the line.

"The deputy chief would like to see you in the morning," the woman said. "Are you available?"

I said that I was. It was my vacation but it was rare to get an audience with the police. The Kilpatrick scandal had the department on a lockdown.

The real press knew that the department solved about one quarter of its cases—a national disgrace—and reporters were kept at arm's length.

After months of being stonewalled, I threatened to sue the department if they did not open their homicide ledger to me. With no legal basis to deny me the records, the brass had finally called me in for the meeting.

I finished my beer, walked buck naked up the hill, kissed my wife and daughter, got dressed and drove back to the city for the meeting.

Among those in attendance were the two men who had put Detective Wright up to the phone with my boss, pressuring him to recant his statement that he was the only detective assigned to the murder of the firefighter Walt Harris.

The deputy police chief sat behind a metallic desk, imperious, heavily muscled beneath a starched dress shirt. There was a window to his right, the blinds drawn to keep the sight of Detroit where it belonged. Outside. The deputy chief squinted anyway.

The lieutenant from the homicide bureau stood off to his side, like a court servant, dressed in an ill-fitting suit that looked as though it belonged on a ventriloquist's doll. His skull was neatly shaved and framed by dark-rimmed spectacles. The lieutenant, despite his rank, had never worked a homicide case in his career.

The deputy chief, for his part, was a political creature, a man who had rapidly scaled the ranks of the department through hard work, a good measure of competence and the uncanny ability to make himself scarce when the shit hit the fan.

The deputy chief had a good shot of making chief one day if he could avoid scandal sticking to him. Not an easy proposition in the Detroit PD.

To him, I represented just another steaming pile positioned between him and the top job.

He thumbed through paperwork, explaining to me in an avuncular tone that the 306 homicide tally was a clerical error attributable to the state police computers.

"So you see the true number is 339, Charlie."

"Now, I'm just a redneck who went to public school," I said, flipping through a folder full of spreadsheets. "But according to my math that leaves another four dozen bodies unaccounted for."

That's when he explained the "back-out" log.

In Detroit police thinking, some homicides just weren't homicides and so they were "backed out," or not counted.

"You see, Charlie, there's homicide and there's murder," the deputy chief explained patiently. "Now, when the medical examiner still says it's a homicide and we go on about our investigation and in the course of our investigation we present documents to the prosecutor's office, they can say it's self-defense. It's ruled medically a homicide. But in the eyes of the prosecutor's office, they will not charge anybody with this. So it's not a murder."

"Like for instance?" I asked.

"Well, let's see," he counted. "There were ten police killings, so those don't count."

He was right about that. The FBI allows killings by police to be backed out of the murder count. Still, it was a shocking number. That made the Detroit Police Department the deadliest in America.

No one had reported this, despite the fact that the department was supposed to be operating under federal supervision for, among other things, the overuse of lethal force.

"And okay, okay, here you go," the deputy chief continued, stabbing his finger at the spreadsheet, certain that he had found a convincing case in his revolver of reason.

"Two brothers were drinking. They got in an argument. One pulled out a knife. So the brother pulled out a knife and killed his brother. I mean, what would you call that?"

"Me?" I said, looking around the room at the assembled brass. "Me? I'd call that a murder."

"I call that insufficient evidence," he said with a straight face.

I understood. Pressured to bring the murder rate down, the police were engaging in nonsensical reclassifications, and it turned out they had been doing it for years. For example, a man named Antonio Bailey suffered a fatal gunshot wound to the head. The medical examiner ruled it a homicide; the police called it suicide. A man named Roland Jordan was found near the highway, beaten to death, the medical examiner said. The police ruled it an accident.

Were the cops systematically undercounting murders? And if detectives were having trouble closing cases, then how many murderers were walking the streets of the Murder Capital?

Walt Harris, the firefighter who died in the arson, was homicide victim no. 288 on the police murder list. Seeing his name, I reached out to an investigator. After I had embarrassed the department with a front-page story about no one looking into Harris's death, a major squad was put together to hunt for his killer. The investigator told me to meet him at a bar on Grand River. It was a scene out of a

Chandler novel. The cop was dressed in a trench coat and porkpie hat even though it was the middle of summer. He drank whiskey neat and a beer chaser even though it was the middle of the morning.

"So your guy, Harris," he said, looking at his shoes. "We got the killer."

"Yeah," I said too loudly. "Who? When?"

"A guy named Darian Dove. A lowlife. Kind of slow. Does odd jobs, that sort of thing. He admits he was paid to torch the house. Says he watched it burn from a nearby gas station. Says the owner, who promised him a new truck, was standing there with him."

"No shit? How'd you find him?"

"Traced the owner's cell phone records to him. Turns out Dove dialed 911. He didn't do it out of decency but because the owner didn't want to burn the house too much, just enough for some insurance dough. The guy's pissed off the owner never gave him the truck."

"That's great news," I said, ordering a congratulatory beer. "I'll get it in the paper tonight."

"No, no you don't," the cop said, grabbing my forearm. "There's a little problem."

"Oh, no. What?"

"I don't think we got him Miranda'd right. We're working on it, so just keep it out of the papers or you'll fuck it up. I'll let you know when."

I was ready to publish the body-count story when the lieutenant called, like some kind of soothsayer.

"I thought we had an understanding, Charlie," he pleaded. "If it's not a technically charged murder, how is it a homicide?"

"How do you change a homicide into a suicide, is what I want to know."

"Fine," he said, hissing like an air hose.

He hung up the phone knowing how it was going to turn out.

The murder story appeared on the front page the next morning with a very safe headline: DETROIT POLICE ROUTINELY UNDERREPORT HOMICIDES.

My work voice mail was full of hate.

Beep: "White men like you, Charlie, sowing discontent, Charlie. I bet you're feeling real comfortable in that little castle you built, Charlie. Well, we coming from the neighborhoods and we gonna burn your castle down, white man. It's gonna be a long, hot summer, Charlie. Watch your ass."

Beep: "What do you expect from niggers? Everything they touch goes to shit. Want to solve the murder problem? Send them back to Africa."

And so forth.

As I was mulling over these friendly salutations, a man who had read my story called me to complain that he was a witness to a murder five years prior and now wanted to come forward, but the police wouldn't give him the time of day.

I called the lieutenant from homicide.

"Oh yeah?" His voice was dripping with contempt. "Have him call me," he said tersely and hung up.

I called the mayor's office for the follow-up story. It's an old newspaper trick. You drop a front-page article. The town gets embarrassed. The mayor promises action. A ribbon is cut and it goes back to business as usual.

But this is Detroit. When I called Mayor Bing's press office, they inexplicably declined comment and told me to call the police. So I called the police.

"We stand by the number, 339," said the new department spokesman. "We're saying that it's not a homicide when two people stab each other and further investigation shows a man was defending himself. So it was a homicide? Who says that?"

"The FBI," I answered.

"Who says the FBI decides?" he snapped. "The bottom line is, if we say it's justifiable, it's not a homicide. More power to the FBI."

I put it in my copy, pressed "send" and walked out to my car, shaking my head.

When I got to my car, I stopped laughing. Somebody had slashed my tire. It could have been random. Probably was. But this was an old Checker taxicab, the big curvy kind you see in old New York movies. It's noticeable in a town where cars don't last five years. I changed the tire and drove home to my nice house in the 'burbs, thinking things were getting out of hand: death threats and racial venom and now a shiv in my tire.

I was going to have to change cars.

The following morning, a woman who had read my follow-up story called to tell me that the man who said he had witnessed a homicide years before was, in fact, a suspect in the murder of her husband.

She claimed he had been released from jail because the witness in that case had mysteriously turned up dead.

I went to the clipping files to see if her story was true. It was.

I laughed to myself. Only in Detroit would a murder suspect call to report a murder suspect and the chief of the homicide squad refuse to take his number.

Soon after, Police Chief James Barren was notified by Mayor Bing that he was fired.

Barren was replaced by Warren Evans, the Wayne County sheriff, who got together with the prosecutor and settled on a revised 2008 murder tally of 375. Baltimore could rejoice. Detroit was once again the Murder Capital.

Evans was a lean, precise, well-groomed dictator. Raised in the Shrine of the Black Madonna, he had a deep and abiding affection for the city of Detroit and believed the city was more important in the American black experience than Harlem itself.

Having said that, Evans knew the city was crumbling and its people fleeing to the suburbs because of marauding criminals who terrorized the citizens. Evans promised to clean up Dodge by doing "whatever it takes"—which meant both busting heads and walking over union rules.

Evans was probably the most competent appointment Bing made in his first term as mayor. And it was an appointment that would come to an appalling and ridiculous end.

As for Barren, the bad news kept coming. The afternoon he was cleaning out his desk, someone was cleaning out his house. It was the third time his home had been burgled. On this occasion, the thieves took a computer, a television set, jewelry and watches.

"That's part of living in Detroit," Barren explained to me when I reached him by phone. "Police resources are sliced to the bone."

No truer words were ever spoken, but citizens were left to wonder why the police department—a week later—assigned four squad cars to escort two hearses to the cemetery.

There weren't human cadavers in the back of the hearses but rather stuffed animals left at the Motown Historical Museum by adoring fans in memory of the late pop star Michael Jackson, who had died of a drug overdose.

There may have been 250 unclaimed dead people at the county morgue, but at least the toys were safe and got a proper burial.

The stuffed animals were laid to rest at Woodlawn Cemetery, near the mausoleum of civil rights icon Rosa Parks.

You Better Get My Loot

THE POLICE CHIEF wasn't the only politico packing his belongings. With the key players in the billion-dollar sludge contract cutting deals and pleading guilty to bribery, the strain was showing on Monica Conyers like a cheap cocktail dress. Judging by her erratic behavior, it was just a matter of time.

The madam city council president found herself denying to me and the rest of the press that her ex-con brother had gotten a no-show city job at her request. She denied, in fact, that he was her brother at all before turning around and admitting that he was in fact her brother.

Sensing she was near the end of her freedom and her threadbare sanity, I called Conyers on her cell phone to get an interview. No answer.

I hung up. My phone rang a few moments later, a return call from the same number.

"Monica?"

"Who's this?" the voice answered.

"Charlie LeDuff."

A long pregnant pause.

"Uhmmmmm . . . my name is Teresa," the voice stammered. "Monica doesn't have this number anymore."

"Jesus, you've got to be kidding me," I said with a laugh. "Monica, I know it's you. It's your voice."

"No, this is Teresa. Sorry." And then Monica hung up.

After that, I thought I would never see her again, except in court. But a few days later, with the hounds of justice barking at her heels, Conyers inexplicably consented to do a cooking show with Joel Kurth, the city hall editor for the *News*—with me working as producer.

Barroom brawls. Groping my testicles. A cooking show before being sent to the federal penitentiary. I don't know why she kept doing what she did. Maybe she was nuts. Maybe she was lonely. Maybe there was a master plan rattling around in her brain that I just couldn't wrap my head around. It hardly mattered. Monica Conyers may have been bad for the people of Detroit City, but she was great copy for readers of the *Detroit News*.

The conceit of the cooking show would be to interview Monica while she prepared fried chicken and sweet potato fries in the kitchen of a bar, all the while lying sweetly about her corruption and fraud.

Appropriately enough, it was held downtown in the Eastern Market at a joint called Butchers. The meal was easily five thousand calories, complete with homemade cookies and ice cream smothered in chocolate sauce. Conyers downed it all with a diet iced tea.

After the filming, I was having a silent cigarette with her out back of the restaurant, near the cobblestone street. It was late June, the flies were buzzing around the grease trap. Monica appeared not to notice them. She was quiet and distracted. Sensing an opportunity, I dialed her number. Her phone rang. She looked at me.

"Teresa my ass," I said. "Monica, I've never stalked you. Why won't you answer my calls?"

"It's a scary time for me, you know?" She looked pale and drawn. A frightened little girl. I almost felt bad for her.

After months of denials, she finally admitted to shaking tens of thousands of dollars and jewelry from people with business before the city council and the pension board on which she served.

The feds had it all—Conyers taking envelopes stuffed with cash, Conyers taking money from a businessman's coat pocket, Conyers walking out on her meals without paying. Among the highlights of the wiretapped conversations played in court:

"You'd better get my loot, that's all I know," Conyers told her aide-de-camp Sam Riddle at one point.

"Don't be telling me to do shit. I ain't no little bitch."

Conyers, the wife of the chairman of the House Judiciary Committee, pleaded guilty to conspiracy to commit bribery. The citizens were stuck paying the tab for her court-appointed lawyer.

BURNT FINGERS

NEVIN WAS FIRED from the fire department for the garbage-picked screen door: charged with dereliction of duty, failure to supervise and conduct detrimental to the department. The men who actually took the door returned to work.

He sued, claiming his dismissal was retaliation for calling department brass a "steaming pile of shit" in the local press and alerting state inspectors to the dangerous levels to which the fire department had sunk.

Nevin won his case, including an award of $5,000 plus back pay, and was ordered returned to duty.

They were celebrating the return of Nevin at the Engine Co. 23 firehouse, so my brother Frankie and I went over to congratulate him ourselves. Frankie brought along a large framed black-and-white photograph he took of the busted toilet inside the firehouse—a gift for Nevin, who nearly broke into song when he unwrapped it.

"That's the prettiest fucking thing I ever got," he said. "A picture of a broken fucking toilet in a broken fucking city."

He was right. It was a pretty picture. An American flag hanging crookedly above the stained commode, a drying mop leaning stiffly against the stall.

It was high art if you actually knew what you were looking at, if you understood the context of where you were standing. If your friend had died and you knew it didn't have to be and you knew what killed him was incompetence and corruption, you might call that photograph of the busted toilet epic poetry. If you knew that this place was sliding toward the drainpipe, a place that your grandfather built, you'd call it sculpture.

Grandpa Nevin's old house was just down the block falling in on itself, toasted like a burnt mattress. And the grandson kept trying anyway: running into burning houses, running out with choking children, trying to save what he could of this place, and he couldn't even keep the flies out of the firehouse because there were no fucking screen doors.

The teapot was burning up on the stove and the town was caving in and his best friend was dead and all Nevin had was this photograph of a toilet with a busted seat and it was the prettiest fucking piece of art he'd ever seen.

"Thanks man, I'm gonna put that right in my living room," he told Frankie.

Nevin set the photo down near the chow table and disappeared upstairs where the bunks and lockers are. I followed him without his knowing. He went straight to Walt's old locker, which had been set up like a religious shrine with his photos and funeral card and tools and turnout gear inside.

Nevin held a cheap cigar in his right knuckles and leaned against Walt's locker door. He rubbed his head where hair used to be. With his left hand he covered his eyes and he cried a little, I think.

. . .

James Mack, the fire official who had led me out of fire headquarters by the elbow a few months before and deposited me into the rain, was now the fire commissioner. I took Nevin's predicament to be a clear message that anyone who got out of line, anyone who appeared in my column space, anyone who was advocating for a change in the department or the way things worked in Wayne County government generally was on the hit list.

So as promised, I started peeling through fire department paperwork looking for the missing screen door money. I requested under the Freedom of Information Act reams and reams of contracts and inspection reports and cashed checks from the Detroit Building Authority, which oversees city construction projects.

Normally, I don't write about paperwork, I write about whiskers and sweat. But it was apparent that the city, the regular people who lived in Detroit, was being destroyed—at best by ineptitude and at worst by graft.

A young, bashful receptionist was assigned to sit with me in a windowless conference room as we went through stacks of contracts. The ventilation system seemed to be broken, which gave the room a suffocating, funeral parlor feel.

The records they gave me were shoddy, invoices billed to wrong addresses, and in many cases paperwork was missing. It would have taken a forensic accountant to sort it all out.

But after hours of random reading, I began to see it: $7 million for doorknobs and faucet handles and screen doors that never saw their way to the firehouses. Money just seemed to vanish in the paper shuffle. An emergency addition needed here. A change order there. A little painting gets done. The rest seemingly disappears.

Take the joint police precinct and firehouse on the city's west side. It began as a $240,000 no-bid contract and ballooned into a $20 million job as far as the paperwork said. Everybody got paid and Detroit did the paying.

The floors in that joint police precinct and firehouse were cracked, the heat didn't work and water pipes to fill the fire engines were forgotten.

They may not have been the Pentagon Papers and they weren't going to win me any Pulitzer Prizes, but the contracts offered a clue as to how this city had been bled to near death over the decades.

I made copies of random reports and toured the firehouses, having to knock at the back doors, because firefighters were afraid to be seen with me in public after what happened to Nevin.

But I was always shown in and always given a fresh cup of coffee. And I was barraged with complaints from the firefighters; their frustration had been corked up like a rancid wine. Few had paid them any mind in years. No reporter in town covered the department as a beat and so I was given the rubber carpet treatment.

I was shown mold, leaking pipes, exposed asbestos insulation, broken toilets, cracked floors, malfunctioning heating units, feces bubbling up from the sewer pipes in the basements. I'd seen better government buildings in the slums of Tijuana.

Nevin and the boys from Engine 23 had told me it was bad, but what I was seeing was worse than the Baghdad fire department, which actually got more than $150 million from the United States government, while Detroit got zero.

After visiting at least a dozen firehouses, I arranged a meeting with the top fire officials down at headquarters in the old brick building. I was led into a room with a large cartoonish mural of firefighters, a mahogany table as large as the mural, and a hyperactive radiator that was whining like a chained dog. The room was a balmy eighty-five degrees. I removed my tie and rolled up my sleeves.

After a few minutes, in walked Commissioner Mack and two underlings—none of them carried so much as a pencil.

"What specific questions do you have?" Mack asked in a dismissive voice, taking a seat. He noticed my tape recorder and forbade me from taping the meeting. "There's no need for that, is there now?" he said with a toothy smile.

"No problem, sir," I said. He did not remember me from the elevator. I showed him some invoices.

Firefighters at Ladder Co. 19 house on Detroit's east side couldn't park their fire trucks in the main house because the floor was unsound, even though the city had set aside nearly a half million dollars to repair it.

"Maybe it was a clerical error," cracked the first underling, insinuating that a clerk simply confused Ladder Co. 19 house for Engine Co. 19 house.

"I thought of that," I said. "The problem is, there is no Engine Co. 19 house, though that firehouse received a quarter million in renovations too."

"Lemme see," she said, snatching for the documents like an opossum at the trash bag. She pawed through the papers a long time before she came up with this: "I don't know what to tell you."

I also had paperwork for Engine Co. 22, which was awarded a half million dollars for a new floor. Problem was that property was last used a decade ago as a Mexican restaurant: the Casa de España. It was now boarded up and falling in. Assuming that too was a clerical error, I couldn't find a new floor at Ladder Co. 22. The pattern was apparent.

"I'll look into it," Mack promised without looking at the documents. "Anything else?"

"Yes, there is," I said chummily, really enjoying the moment. "The Fire Training Academy was awarded $1.5 million for a new training tower. There is no new training tower. The money disappeared."

The money may not seem like much considering the size of the automobile bailouts, but it was enough to reoutfit the entire department with bunker gear and breathing apparatus and homing alarms. The second underling, who looked freakishly like his superior, with both the toothy smile and the shorn skull, explained that the tower project was abandoned and the money was reallocated to put a million-dollar roof on another building.

However, there was no paper trail showing a stop-work order on the training tower or what became of the other $600,000, I told him.

"It's air," the look-alike underling explained with the smile. "That million was allocated but it's not there. In the case of canceled jobs, there is no paper trail. I guess you can infer a paper trail. That's how many things go down here."

Mack stopped the meeting short. "Make a list of questions, we'll get back to you," he said.

I smiled, gathered up my paperwork and headed for the door.

"Either someone let you in these firehouses, which is against department regulations, or you've got X-ray vision," the first underling said to me on my way out.

"Something like that," I said. "It's easy to see inside when there's no screen doors."

Then I turned to Mack, who was escorting me to the door. "You remember me?"

He gave me a once-over. "I can't say I do, Mr. LeDuff."

"One thing about me, sir," I told him. "I keep my promises."

It was bullshit but it felt good to say it. Because after I wrote the story up and published it in the paper . . . nothing happened. Nobody was fired. No investigation was started. No firehouse got fixed. Seemed like nobody gave a shit except the parakeet using the Metro section as a septic field.

TWENTY BUCKS

IT WAS LATE FALL, nearly a year since Harris's death. Outside the courthouse window, leaves were falling from the trees, whipping in the streets.

Inside the courtroom, Darian Dove sat in the witness chair with his chin buried in his chest and mumbled the events of November 15. They began with a can of gasoline and ended when a roof collapsed on Walt Harris.

At the defendant's table, Mario Willis sat impassively in a jail-green jumpsuit as Dove recounted how Willis had hired him to burn up the house "a little bit" for an insurance job.

Dove, a worn-at-the-heel handyman, had cut a plea deal. He got a hamburger and seventeen years in prison in exchange for his testimony against his boss Willis.

Willis, whose gold-framed spectacles nicely set off the green prison attire, presented himself to the court as a business sharp and man of God who orbited in the same universe as Mayor Kilpatrick. He maintained his innocence.

Not according to the handyman. According to him, Willis had picked him up around 2:30 A.M. and they stopped at a Gratiot Avenue service station to buy gasoline.

"He paid," Dove mumbled. "I didn't have no money."

From there, they drove to Kirby Street, where Willis waited in his vehicle while Dove went to set fire to the house.

"He called me on my cell phone," Dove said, so quietly that the judge told him to speak up. "He called me on my cell phone. He said: 'What's taking so long?'"

Dove set the fire, then he tried to put it out with his shirt because the boss didn't want the whole thing burned down in case he wanted to burn it again a couple months later. It was an insurance job, Dove said. He'd set a fire at the same house a few years before, whereupon Willis had collected $20,000. He never made repairs to the house and the city never required him to do so.

But the handyman couldn't get the flames under control this time by waving a shirt at it. A piece of timber broke loose from the ceiling and struck him on the head, knocking him down.

After collecting his senses, he ran out to the boss's vehicle and they drove to a gas station where Dove called 911 from a pay phone to report the fire.

Harris's widow sat impassively in the gallery, leaning into the shoulder of firefighter Jimmy Montgomery while Nevin draped a broad hand across her shoulder.

"He said he was going to buy me a new truck when he got the money," Dove continued, mumbling into his wiry beard. "He never bought me nothing, though. He gave me twenty bucks is all."

"How much?" the prosecutor asked.

"Twenty bucks," he repeated.

The courtroom gasped.

CHEAPER THAN A MOVIE

ARSONISTS DO THEIR best work at night. As do murderers. And so it stands to reason that homicide dicks should work the graveyard shift. But it's a bad thing to give your number to these types of cops, because they like to ruin your sleep. One evening, homicide detective Sgt. Mike Martel called me while I was curled up on the couch. He said he had a scene I might be interested in. I slid my trousers on and drove to the southwest side.

There was a doctor or something who had his Mercedes-Benz ruined by his brains splattered all over the leather interior.

"Look at it," the detective said, shining his flashlight on the dead man. He was slumped over the wheel almost like he was leaning to change the radio station. From the passenger side you could see his teeth. All of his teeth. Half his face was gone. Glass stuck to his golf shirt. His shoes were in need of a competent polish.

"Did you bring a camera?" the detective asked.

"No."

"Too bad. Good picture." He pulled off the rubber gloves from his large, nail-bitten hands. He slipped them into his suit pocket. It was hot but he still wore a hat. A porkpie with a feather in it. It looked ridiculous but that's a Detroit murder thing. The homicide cops wear hats. Still, his hat didn't fit and I never knew Martel to wear one. He must have borrowed it. He was clowning me on the crime set. Murder does that to a man's mind if he stares into it long enough.

"Shouldn't try painting the town red in this part of town," he lectured the corpse, pantomiming pity for the dead man in the expensive car who didn't really deserve any. "It's usually your own blood that gets used for paint."

He turned to me. "You hungry?"

We sat in a local diner, a rundown joint with walls the color of an old man's teeth. I watched the detective tear into a chili dog. He weighed 350 pounds and was trying that meat-only diet.

"The whole shit is corrupt from top to bottom," he said through his mustache and a mouthful of dog. "Cops to judges. The fucking radios in the cars don't even work. Why you think so many guys are leaving the department?"

And then he launched into the craziest story of true-life murder I'd ever been told.

"You should look into this one, it's totally fucked."

In January 2008, a teenage street tough named Deandre Woolfolk made plans to avenge a failed hit on his boss, Darnell Cooley, a reputed drug dealer who was lying in a hospital in a coma.

Woolfolk tried to enlist the help of a neighborhood mope named Perry to be the getaway driver.

Perry declined, insisting he had to work that night. But Perry never went to work. Perry didn't even have a job. Instead, Perry went to the intersection of Fenkell and Wyoming, where he had been told the hit would take place, to watch. Before Perry arrived, however, the thirty-four-year-old picked up his sixteen-year-old brother and three teenage girls, including fifteen-year-old Martha Barnett.

It was two A.M. on a school night. They went shopping for Slurpees and snack cakes.

"It was cheaper than a movie," the detective said, launching into his second dog. That's the same thing Nevin told me about arson, I thought. *Cheaper than a movie.*

In any event, that evening's entertainment didn't turn out to be as cheap as he figured. Perry either forgot or did not know that the intended target of the hit drove a black Jeep—just like his.

And when Woolfolk and his hit squad came careening around the corner, they did not stop at the Jeep to inquire. One opened up with an AK-47. Woolfolk, sitting in the front passenger seat, raised a 9 mm pistol, pointed and pulled the trigger.

"What's going on?" little Martha screamed.

When the smoke cleared, little Martha Barnett was dead with a gunshot wound to the head.

Woolfolk got away for a couple months, until he was swept up in a dope raid on the city's west side. He was arrested among a cache of weapons and narcotics.

Two days after his arrest, Woolfolk was interrogated by Sergeant Martel. During that taped interrogation, he was read his Miranda rights. And on that tape he admitted that he was in the car when the girl was murdered and that he had indeed tried to shoot but that his gun jammed.

"How can I be responsible for a gun I didn't fire?" he asked.

The driver and the shooter with the AK-47 were convicted of

first-degree murder, but Woolfolk's lawyer—who was married to a judge—argued that his client had repeatedly asked to speak with a lawyer before he confessed but was denied one by detectives.

The judge believed him and threw out his confession on the grounds that Woolfolk probably had asked for a lawyer since he knew the legal system so well.

With little other evidence, the prosecutor was forced to drop the charges.

Woolfolk walked.

Fast forward six months. Robert Alexander had gone to Arturo's Jazz Club in Southfield, a suburb of Detroit, to celebrate his thirty-third birthday. He went with a group of guys from the barbershop and their girlfriends. Among them was his best friend, Anthony Alls.

Also there was Woolfolk, along with kingpin Darnell Cooley, who had gotten over his coma and was feeling better.

The evening began as a good one. Champagne was flowing, the music was sweet. Then someone from Woolfolk's table spoiled the evening by fondling one of the women at Alexander's table. Alexander, a large man weighing more than 250 pounds, went over to straighten it out.

When police arrived, they found Alexander lying amid upset tables, a broken bottle and his own blood. He was faceup, unconscious and gasping for air. Then he died.

There was only one willing witness. His friend Anthony Alls. And Alls put the finger squarely on Woolfolk and Cooley and a third man named Eiland Johnson.

A few weeks later Alls was leaving his job at a Detroit barbershop. He walked around the corner and opened the hood of his '88 Bronco. This was the usual routine for Alls. The power-steering pump leaked like a sandbag, and before he would start the motor, he would fill the reservoir with fluid. He was meaning to take it in to the mechanic to get it fixed.

While Alls was stooped over the quarter panel, someone approached from behind and unloaded six shots into his back. Alls was spun around by the force of the barrage and took a seventh in the chest. He stumbled backward and collapsed on the sidewalk. Then he died.

Instead of the mechanic, Alls went to the morgue. The killer calmly walked around the corner and disappeared.

"He'd been subpoenaed to appear in court just five hours before he was murdered," Martel said, spearing his chili fries with a plastic fork. So much for the meat-only diet, I was thinking.

"For whatever reason, they provided no protection for him," he said.

Nobody got a look at Alls's killer.

Two days later, police arrested a man breaking into his ex-girl-friend's house. The man, not wanting to do another stretch in prison, said he had information on Alls's murder. The man said he did paid hits himself and had information on a handful of other murders as well. He wanted to be an informant. And this was all on police videotape.

"Do you know Alls was scheduled to go into the police academy?" Martel asked me.

"No shit?" I said, writing the detail down on a napkin.

"No shit," he said, slurping his Diet Pepsi. "He was basically a cop."

But before Martel could put the informant to work—get him wired and get him back on the streets—a junior prosecutor turned the hit man's taped interrogation over to the judge and the defense lawyers.

Without a living, breathing witness, the prosecutor was trying to show that Alls was killed to keep him quiet. This, he hoped, would convince the judge to allow the dead man's statement as evidence in court.

Martel said he pleaded with the prosecutor to stall for a few more weeks while he used the hit man to gather information on the murders by wiring him up.

He even begged the prosecutor to call in sick to court.

The prosecutor refused.

"I told that asshole to give me thirty days and we can get all them fuckers," Martel said, scanning the joint for eavesdroppers. We were the only ones in there except the fry cook and the girl at the register. They were watching TV. I noticed Martel had dribbled chili on his tie.

"The prick refused. Flat out refused. Said he wasn't going to break the rules of the court. So he gets to be a Boy Scout and we're going to get some very bad men back on the street. Motherfucker."

He picked up the check. When a cop picks up a check, you know he's serious.

"You want me to have him call you?"

"Who?"

"The hit man, my informant. He's scared for his life because his name is now out on the street."

"Call me? Yeah, sure. Give him my cell number, I guess."

Suddenly I was in the middle of a gangster picture and I didn't have the script.

BIG MARTHA

As for Little Martha Barnett, I tracked the end of her story to a linen closet on the city's west side, where her grandmother kept her remains, too poor to bury the ashes.

"All the pain that man caused," the grandmother, a decent, churchgoing woman also named Martha Barnett, told me at her dining room table about Woolfolk. "Why? Why was he still allowed to walk 'round?"

Big Martha's house held the choking, musty smell of fear so common in Detroit. Fear to open the door or the windows. Fear that someone might decide to break in and take the TV—or a life.

Inside the linen closet near the bathroom, above the rolls of toilet paper and a bag of dirty laundry, Barnett kept the ashes of Little Martha in a brass urn in a plastic bag.

Big Martha, seventy-three, paid her rent with a Social Security check and lived with her infirm daughter Sharon—Little Martha's mother.

Dressed in checked pajama bottoms at four in the afternoon,

Sharon shuffled in and out of the bedroom where her daughter used to sleep, listening to a radio, occasionally going to the stove to light her cigarette. The first time she emerged from the bedroom and held her head over the flame, she caught her wig on fire but patted it out without panic and shambled back to the bedroom.

The second time she emerged, she lit the cigarette without incident, and before going back into the bedroom she turned to me and said with a vacant stare: "I should have stayed in school. Oh well, it's never too late, right? I could always go back to trade school. Learn a little skill or something."

Sharon must have been frozen in that bedroom for twenty years. What trades? It was all gone, honey. All gone, including your daughter.

"That's a real good idea," I lied.

Pacified, Sharon shuffled back to her radio.

Martha sat at a kitchen table covered with a peeling plastic cloth, a painting of the Last Supper hanging on the wall behind her and next to that a glass menagerie filled with owls and eagles and a photo of the Obama family, which was striking to me since there were no photographs of her own kin.

"I wished I might be able to leave this big city here," Big Martha said in a thick Mississippi accent. Like many religious women raised in the South, she believed God reveals His divine plan to her through dreams.

"I been having a dream of that fishing hole in the country outside Greenville, Mississippi. That's where I come from. I believe the Almighty is calling me away from here, Mr. Charlie. He got something else left for me. He want me to go home."

"Please don't call me Mr. Charlie," I said.

"Okay then, Charlie. I been wishing I never come up here.

Trapped in the ghetto like this. People running wild. My grandbaby dead. Me too poor to bury her."

Big Martha retrieved the urn, set it on the table. The polishing machine had scarred the facing.

Big Martha began crying. All the pain that little girl got caught up in. All the pain Woolfolk caused. All the pain we all carry around. She cried until Sharon came out to light another cigarette.

"I know my grandbaby's in a better place," Big Martha said. "Absent from the body. Present with the Lord," she said, quoting the New Testament.

I thought about my sister, Nicky. I would go around the part of town where she died rather than drive through it. I avoided it not out of fear, but sadness. I couldn't face it. It was my own linen closet. I guess that's why dogs don't put their snouts in the fire. Too much pain. I hadn't even visited the grave where she and her daughter lay.

Big Martha talked about Little Martha's funeral.

"So many people was there, so many young people. I didn't know all those young people loved her so much. Well, in the middle of the funeral, during the songs, the funeral director stopped the music right there in the middle of the service, and he brought me in the back room and was asking how I was gonna pay for it. I didn't rightly know. I should have passed the hat right there. Everybody would have given, praise God. But I didn't pass the hat. So I had her cremated. I had to borrow and beg just to do that. Even her father chipped in. They charged me seven thousand dollars for the casket and everything."

"What happened to the casket?" I asked.

"They told me they burned it too."

"That's a lot of money for nothing."

"I know, but people like me's sorta dumb in death, honey. We ain't got much on this earth. You want to send your people out

EVIDENCE DETROIT
DANNY WILCOX FRAZIER

LIFE AND DEATH AND LIMBO.

DANNY FRAZIER HAS SEALED THEM ALL

IN THE BELL JAR OF HIS SECRET LITTLE CAMERA.

THIS IS HIS PORTRAIT OF DETROIT IN ITS DECISIVE MOMENT:

SMOKE AND SOOT AND BLOOD.

DETROIT — AN ALMOST IMPOSSIBLE PLACE. AN AMERICAN

PLACE FROM WHICH AMERICANS CAST AWAY THEIR EYES.

BUT GIANTS THROW LONG SHADOWS AND

HAVING NOTICED IT OUT THERE IN THE CORN, FRAZIER

JUMPED IN HIS RATTLETRAP, TOOK A ROOM IN SOME

DUMP ON JEFFERSON AVE. AND

GOT DOWN TO THE WORK OF STARING CLEANLY INTO IT.

WHAT HE HAS CAPTURED HERE IS THE CITY'S MARROW

IN 6 X 6 CHEMICAL GRAIN.

THE OLD SOOTY SMOKESTACKS OF A FACTORY LONG GONE.

THE OLD FLINTY MAN NOT FAR BEHIND.

A SEXPOT DRAGGING HER HEELS THROUGH RUBBLE.

A RAKE IN SILK. DEATH IN SATIN AND MAHOGANY.

THE COLD STEEL OF

THE EXAMINER'S TABLE. A PEOPLE HOLDING TIGHT.

ALL RIGHT HERE ON FILM, DANNY BOY. ALL RIGHT HERE.

GOOD GOD AND WAR,

IT'S ALL RIGHT HERE.

CHARLIE LEDUFF

Summer Night, Belle Isle

ABANDONED DOLLHOUSE, MIDTOWN

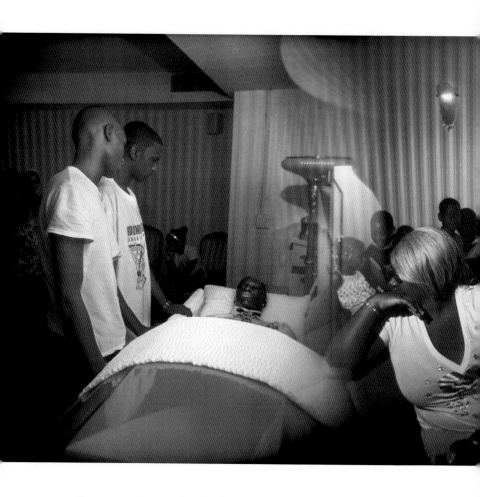

FUNERAL OF AN INNOCENT BOY, EAST SIDE

GOD + WAR, EAST SIDE

Packard Plant, East Side

BED AND SHOE, WEST SIDE

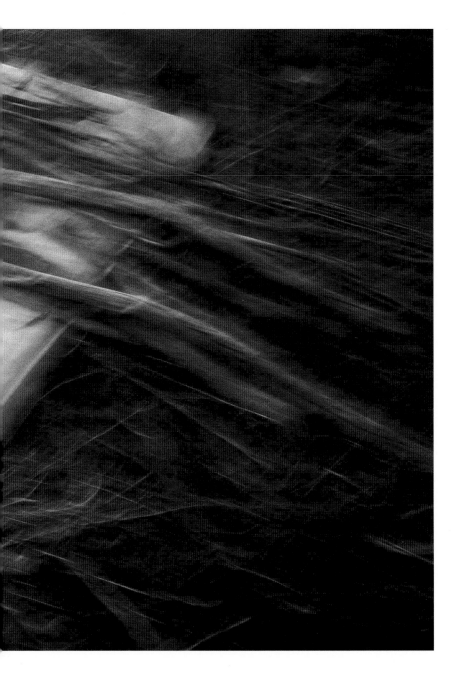

Four Alarms, East Side

Unclaimed Dead, County Morgue, Midtown

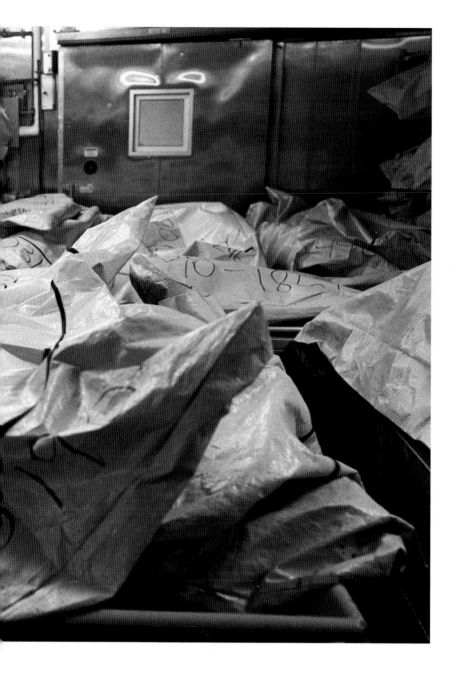

PRAYING, EAST SIDE

CHILD, EAST SIDE

FIREMEN, EAST SIDE

FRONT STEPS, SOUTHWEST SIDE

Empty Factory, East Side

FIRE NEXT DOOR, EAST SIDE

proper. The news channels they says they was gonna help me, but they never did. Never helped a thing. Not that I expected them to. They took all of the pictures I had of my baby and they never brought 'em back. Said they was gonna help, and all they did was call my little lamb a prostitute and things like that on the news. It hurt something terrible, the way it all happened."

She cried a little more. Seeing a half-filled ashtray, I lit a cigarette and waited out the tears.

"Well, can't nobody hurt her no more," Big Martha said, composing herself. "She's with Jesus Christ. Better place. We all going to that place, that's a birthday none of us is going to miss."

Barnett came to Detroit in 1977 by way of Chicago. Her son, Clarence Jr., was murdered in 1979 when he was thrown from a second-story window in the Cass Corridor. He's buried in Belleville, way out by the airport; she knows not where.

Her husband, Clarence, died of lung cancer in 1994 and is buried at the Sacred Heart Cemetery, part of the old Polish church located in what is now a rough east side neighborhood. The priest there lives in the rectory, behind an iron door.

Clarence's grave is unacknowledged. Barnett said she paid for a stone when Clarence died, but the salesman ran off with the $300. As it happened, the stone salesman cheated a lot of poor people before he died.

She ran through her finances: "HUD wants to move me out of this house, put me on the east side with the criminals and hooligans. They want to sell this house and fix it up. I only pay sixty-one dollars a month. Where am I gonna get the extra money? I keep applying for Section 8, and they keep denying me 'cause I'm old, I guess—and I'm gonna die if they just ignore me and I suppose I won't have no headstone neither."

I didn't know what to say. I wanted to do something for this woman. She was my forebear in some way, my auntie, trapped and scared and bunking with a zombie. I offered to find her the money to bury Little Martha.

"That'd be a beautiful thing, Mr. Charlie."

"Please, just Charlie."

"Okay then, Charlie. But you know something, Charlie? I'd much rather have a car," Martha said hopefully. "I mean, to get around, you know? Maybe a van. Can you help me with a van? White people got nice cars for sale in they yards. I'm sure you know a lot of white people with a van."

Sharon walked by and lit a half-smoked menthol on the stove again. Then she silently went back to her radio. She forgot to shut off the flame.

Kiss the Babies

I was in my underwear, shaving cream on my face, a razor in my hand. I was getting dressed for my aunt's funeral.

That's when a man called me. He spoke fast and he spoke as though he had matriculated at the University of Jailhouse Law School.

"So-and-So told me to give you a call," he said without introducing himself, without so much as a good morning.

"Who's So-and-So?" I asked the voice, confused. "Who is this?"

"Our mutual friend on that barbershop job," the voice said. "He told me you might want to talk."

I quickly put it together. It was the hit man caught on an interrogation tape saying he would be willing to wear a wire to send the Black Mafia to prison.

Understanding now, I set down the razor and picked up a pen. The hit man whined that he had been aggrieved, that the assistant prosecutor broke all notions of protocol when he turned the interrogation tape over to the defense attorneys working for the very people he was snitching on.

"Me and my family's dead, know what I'm saying? I mean, the first witness got killed," he shouted. "The prosecutor's desperate for a case, but they can't even use that tape. I could have been lying. It's hearsay. If they subpoena me, I ain't saying shit. I'm taking the Fifth. Who's gonna protect me? I'm fucking dead. I ain't going out without a gun battle. I promise. There's gonna be a war."

"I didn't know there were rules in the murder business," I said to him.

"Gangsters dying, that's part of the game. But innocent people? No."

He was worried that the "Family" now knew his identity and was going to kill his children, him and his dog.

A dollop of shaving cream dripped to the floor. I wiped it out with a toe.

The hit man said he was going to hurt the prosecutor if his own children got hurt.

"I wouldn't do that," I said.

"What do you think I should do?" he asked me.

"Get out of Dodge," I said lamely. Like I said, I've never been in a gangster picture. I was grasping for dialogue here.

"That ain't gonna work, they'll find me," he said. "There's gonna be a war."

"Then I'm talking to a dead man," I said.

"You probably right."

"Call So-and-So," I said. "But just calm down and don't do anything stupid. I gotta go to a funeral. I'll call you later. Just don't go killing anybody."

"Aw, man, I'm fucked."

"Yeah, you are."

"If anything happens to my family," the hit man warned me again, "that fucking prosecutor, he can kiss the babies."

I hung up the phone and went back to the bathroom to finish shaving. I'd have to call the prosecutor, I figured. If I wasn't legally obligated to do so, I suppose I was morally. Even if the guy was a fucking tool.

Grandma

My wife and I loaded up the baby in the SUV and drove to my aunt's funeral in a rural corner of Oakland County, where the land rolls like a ship on the swells. A boat, a house, a lake, a foreclosure sign.

"Jesus, it's Whitey McWhiteville out here," my wife said distractedly, noticing a white-faced lawn jockey. My woman is a white girl who grew up in Detroit—not the suburbs—which makes her a special kind of white person.

"Have some respect," I barked at her. I don't know why. Maybe it was the idea of the funeral. My people don't handle them very well. There is usually a drunk screaming from an upstairs window, like a stewed sailor on night watch. Sometimes it is a fistfight. One time, a cousin threw a beer bottle at his brother's casket as it was lowered down the hole, screaming that his brother could keep the dime deposit.

I turned up the radio. Manfred Mann was singing, the blackest-sounding white band there probably is. Blue, black and white, can't we get anything right? An appropriated sound, of course, but righteous enough in its own way.

The funeral for my aunt was weird in the fact that it wasn't weird. It was normal. It was white. It started on time. Everyone wore a tie and jacket. Aunt Marilyn, my father's sister, had raised the ultimate American family. A husband of forty-nine years, seven children, twenty-two grandchildren or something like that. No divorce. No death by misadventure. Catholic to the point of evangelical. Her progeny lining up single file to each place a rose in a vase. It was simply odd in its normalcy, its clean-scrubbed sweetness. Who were these people? Where was their bitterness? Their bite? Their whiskers? They couldn't possibly belong to me.

And then a brassy woman stepped out of a dark corner.

"Hi, Charlie?"

"Yes?" I had never seen her before.

"I'm your long-lost Aunt Debbie."

I stood there blankly. She was a well-put-together blonde in a black dress, with red lipstick. A smoker, I thought, by the sound of her voice.

"Your father's half sister?" she offered helpfully. "Your grandmother, she was my mother. Betty? I'm your father's half sister."

"Her name was Betty?"

"Yes, your father's mother. We had the same mother. Betty."

"Betty what?"

"Well, first Betty Lancour. And then Betty LeDuff when she married your father's dad. And then Betty Zink when she married my dad. She died when she was thirty-five years old. Alone."

"Those are a lot of names."

"Yeah, they are."

"How did she die?"

"A heart attack, I think."

"Oh."

"How is your father?"

"I haven't talked to him in a decade," I told my new Aunt Debbie. "Not since my sister's funeral. She was thirty-five too."

"Oh, wow," Aunt Debbie said with an eyebrow.

Like a gossip with a secret, Aunt Debbie wasted little time telling me her son's girlfriend just had her feet amputated because of a virus and that the muffler just fell off her car, making it difficult to fulfill her job, which was to shuttle around the Amish back in Pennsylvania.

This was more like my family. I liked her.

Grandma Betty died alone. Who was she? And who was Grandpa, for that matter? It occurred to me, especially now that I was back in Detroit, that for a man who had spent his entire professional life crisscrossing the planet asking others the most pointed and personal questions, I didn't really know much about my family. Or myself. A boat without an anchor, bobbing across the shores of Whitey McWhiteville.

I eventually found Grandma Betty in the municipal archives.

The radio dispatcher sent scout car no. 10-1 to see about a dead woman, according to the police report. It was 3:35 in the afternoon on March 8, 1956. It was cold outside. Patrolman Mitchell Adamek found a youngish woman lying dead in the back bedroom of Apartment 207 at 2665 Gladstone, on the west side of Detroit, near the Sacred Heart Seminary. She was dressed in a slip, nothing more. There were no visible signs of violence to her body. Adamek contacted the homicide squad anyway.

On the dressing table was a bottle of Anacin tablets, a bottle of

Bufferin tablets, a bottle of nose drops and a bottle of codeine cold remedy in liquid form. In the corner stood John W. Migan, a narrow-shouldered dentist who, at the age of thirty-four, was still living with his mother. He told Adamek that he had been dating the woman for the better part of three years and that he had last seen her about two A.M., when he dropped her off after an evening of spirited partying.

When they were done having a good time, Migan went home to his mother. He returned later that afternoon to find his girlfriend dead.

The woman, Betty Zink, was my grandmother, but as I began digging into her story, I realized she could have been my sister.

It seemed to me looking over her police report that the dead don't take their sorrows and confusion with them, they pass them on like watches and amulets.

Born Betty J. Freed in 1920 to a traveling salesman and a Chippewa Indian woman from Mackinac Island, my grandmother had married and divorced twice in her short life. Her first husband was an elegant, swarthy-skinned man named Royal LeDuff, my grandfather. She bore him two children—my father, Roy Jr., and Marilyn—before the marriage ended in divorce. She then married Robert Zink and bore him two children, Debbie and Bob. That marriage also rapidly dissolved, Betty divorcing herself of Zink and his fists.

By all accounts, she was a fantastically handsome woman, with dark brown hair, gray eyes and a full, curvaceous figure. A door-to-door saleslady, according to the death certificate.

But she was wild and ill equipped for the domestic life. Both sets of children would end up living with their fathers while Betty lived with her demons. She danced with the liquor bottle and dined with barbiturates. The coroner determined her cause of death to be heart failure, but he did not perform toxicology tests. He did note, however, that her liver was in an advanced state of failure.

More than fifty years had passed since her death, and no one had ever mentioned her name to me. No photographs had been passed down, no story. A ghost in the attic. A beautiful woman who was haunted by something unknown to all but herself. A woman who medicated herself into a slow oblivion, to the point of failing organs. A woman who met a dark and sad death, just as her granddaughter Nicole would.

Why had no one spoken about any of this until a long-lost aunt emerged from a dark corner of a cold Catholic church to tell me?

I asked this of my father when he called after hearing through the family telegraph that I was nosing around in the past. I hadn't spoken to him in about ten years. In fact, I hadn't spoken to him probably more than a dozen times in my life, and then it was usually at funerals and family functions. We didn't know much about each other beyond the fact that we shared a name and blood. I told him it didn't seem natural that his mother and his daughter never knew each other's names.

"You've got to understand the thing about this family," he told me. "We were all just pieces of everything, there is no whole there. Nobody really knows the truth."

I was beginning to understand, now that I was home in Detroit, that things are rarely what they seem—they're an amalgam, a fictionalized version of the truth served up to suit people's needs and help them get on with the difficult business of living.

It is like that in most places, I suppose, with most families.

After listening to my father's recollections of his mother, our conversation turned to his father, my grandpa Roy LeDuff. I had always been told that LeDuff was a Cajun name, with its roots in the swamps of Louisiana. This is what my father had been told too. I would come to find out this was a lie.

GRANDPA

MY GRANDPA FIRST touched the woman who would become his
second wife some evening in 1951. They drank and danced and the
buds of a midlife romance bloomed.

The exact date of their rendezvous is lost in time, but it is quite
certain they did not meet on a Monday night. Monday night was
"colored" night at the Vanity Ballroom, located on the east side near
my mother's old flower shop. Monday was the only night blacks
were allowed in the joint.

And Roy LeDuff, my grandfather, was not black.

Not anymore.

LeDuff is a Creole name—belonging to a culture of people with
mixed blood, black and white. In the racial arithmetic of America,
that means black.

Imagine my surprise when, peeling through old government
documents looking for some clue to the LeDuff arrival in Detroit, I
put my thumb on the 1920 U.S. Census, in which my grandfather,
Royal, is listed as an eight-year-old "M"—mulatto.

I could hardly believe it. Here I was, a middle-aged man wandering about in a city where just about every major narrative since the Civil War had been played out in black and white, only to find out what I'd been told about my grandfather's past was false.

I was told there may have been some mixing of the races in a distant wing of my family, and every LeDuff I had ever met was the color of caramel. But the fact that Grandpa himself was born black and died a white man blew me away. Not only did my blood track to the woodlands of the Great Lakes and the Celtic shores of France, but to the Gold Coast of Africa too. The African Diaspora and the Great Migration could be traced through my own family, and it was written on paper.

I sat in my basement smoking cigarettes and looking at an old sepia photograph of my great-grandmother I'd recently been given by a distant relative, wondering how the story of Detroit had come to this point, with me being the palest black man in Michigan.

The name LeDuff, as far as it goes in the United States, can be traced to an eighteenth-century "free man of color" from New Orleans named Jacques LeDuff, whose forebears had come from Brittany, on the coast of France, and on the slave galleons from Africa.

He was a well-to-do man for a time. Although he was colored he lived in an upscale white neighborhood, unheard of in colonial America. Fashioning himself as a gentleman farmer, he also broke ground on a 340-acre plantation in the wilderness southwest of New Orleans that was managed by his slaves.

But alas, as quickly as he earned the silver, he spent it. The War of 1812 came and Jacques found himself a man perpetually in trouble with the bill collectors. He lost his land and his house servant Claude, who was taken away and sold to satisfy a $100 debt.

His son Honoré—the product of Jacques' marriage to Josephine Dupar, a free black woman, or *negresse libre*—was also a veteran of the War of 1812. But lacking an inheritance from his father, Jacques, Honoré moved his family from New Orleans to Pointe Coupée Parish, about twenty-five miles northeast of Baton Rouge, a fertile farming plain between the Mississippi and Atchafalaya rivers.

There, the LeDuff clan lived along the Mississippi River as farmers, coopers and carpenters and spoke what over a couple generations evolved into a Creole French dialect.

Honoré had many children, including Honoré Jr., who sired Donatien, an illiterate sharecropper who himself fathered six boys and a girl. Among them was Henry, my great-grandfather. According to the 1900 census, he was a ten-year-old farm laborer, unable to read or write. Fair-skinned, Henry was listed as "M"—mulatto.

By 1910, Henry had married Inez Porche, a privileged Creole girl who could read and write both English and French. According to his 1917 draft registration, Henry was employed as a carpenter by Inez's family. It appears that Henry, something of a hustler, may have shown up to his draft registration appointment in a cast, making him unfit for war service. In any event, he did not sign his own draft card. The man who signed the name for Henry listed him as "Negro."

At this point, Henry disappeared on the train headed north. He left in the colored car. He left his wife and two sons in a boardinghouse at 110 Plum Street in East Baton Rouge with no visible means of support. Inez and her boys—Earle and Royal, my grandfather—were documented in the 1920 census as mulatto.

Meanwhile, Henry resurfaced in Detroit, one of the millions of blacks who would make their way north to the industrial yards to earn a new life and escape the Jim Crow South. Henry accomplished this in a decidedly curious way.

He took a room at the boardinghouse of Alfred Ingersol, a white machinist at a motor factory. Henry's occupation was listed as "carpentry—auto factory."

Now living a new life, he began constructing a new history. He told the census clerk that his mother was born in Paris and spoke only French. But she was actually a homely mulatto about four feet tall and three feet wide who spoke Creole.

He also told the clerk that he was a white man, and the clerk dutifully wrote it down: "W."

The Motor City was booming then, thanks to men like Henry Ford and the Dodge brothers. In 1925, Detroit's factories employed more than 300,000 people. And thanks to Prohibition and the city's proximity to the liquor distilleries of Canada, another 50,000 were employed in the illicit sale of alcohol. There was money everywhere, and people arrived by the trainload to get theirs. Of those, 120,000 were black Southerners, an epic shift in American demographics known as the Great Migration.

Men and women with histories they were free to erase and reconstruct. How many truths were buried in those years? In Detroit, who really knows? Growing up in the suburbs, they taught us nothing except that one hot day in 1967, the blacks went crazy and burned down the most beautiful city in America and the whites had to leave.

The adults never told us why.

In the Detroit factories, blacks got the worst jobs: at the foundries and grinding tables and paint shops. Because he was now white, Henry was able to work as a carpenter.

In 1924, the LeDuff family reunited in Detroit. Inez and her sons left Baton Rouge by train, traveling in the segregated "colored" cars.

Henry gave his wife a new house on Birwood Street on the city's west side. He also gave her a new child, a case of syphilis and a frying pan in the face when she complained about it.

He gave her one more thing: a new identity. The 1930 Census shows the family living at 14103 Birwood Street, in a Dutch colonial that Henry built with his own hands. The census also shows that the copper-skinned LeDuff clan, a family who had for nearly two centuries been recorded in American government records as either mulatto, Negro or black, had magically been scrubbed "W"—white—hiding the secret among the hordes of swarthy Italians and Greeks and southern Europeans who had also descended upon Detroit.

Henry went by the name Frenchy. It may seem outrageous from today's perspective that a man should dislike his lot so much that he would lie about his blood. But it doesn't seem outrageous to me. Consider Frenchy's time. Detroit was little better than the South for a man with African ancestry. If Henry had admitted he was black, then restrictive—and legal—real estate covenants would have banned him from owning property on Birwood or renting outside the squalid ghettos like Black Bottom or Paradise Valley.

The year Great-Grandma got off the train—1924—a Ku Klux Klan–endorsed candidate was elected mayor of Detroit. Charles Bowles could not take office, however, because it was a write-in campaign and so many of his supporters had misspelled his name that 17,000 ballots were disallowed. During that campaign there were mass marches of Klan supporters—40,000 strong in the city. They even burned crosses on the steps of City Hall.

A few months later, a black man, Dr. Ossian Sweet, had the temerity to move into a white neighborhood on the city's east side. A mob set upon his house and the doctor fired into the crowd, killing a white man. Sweet was defended by noted attorney Clarence Darrow and acquitted of murder by an all-white jury. Still, Dr. Sweet knew better than to press his luck. He left the house. The Sweet incident was the stuff of national headlines and my great-grandmother— much darker than her husband and able to read a newspaper—must have known about the white mobs and the burning crosses.

Great-Grandma LeDuff was said to have had few friends. She threw no parties and rarely came out of her house. She knew she did not belong there.

Looking back, I can't blame Great-Grandpa Henry or Great-Grandma Inez for passing themselves off as some sort of ethnic whites. Henry couldn't have made his life otherwise. A drop of African blood was enough to condemn a man to eternal poverty. Like his grandfather Jacques, he simply found the white neighborhoods preferable.

Henry's son, my grandfather Royal, excelled at mathematics, was considered an excellent dancer and was something of a dandy, with his straightened hair, pencil mustache and taste for expensive clothing. Roy hated his father, Henry, who was surly and an angry drinker, and when he told his own narrative, my grandfather always began it in 1933, the year, I imagine, that he was emancipated from his father's shadow and began working at the post office.

Henry died in 1951, the same year that Grandma Betty Zink died alone, the same year my Grandpa Roy met Betsy Steele at the Vanity Ballroom. Roy and Betsy were married a year later. Roy brought his two children from his previous marriage to Betty Zink, including my father. Betsy gathered up her six children from a previous marriage, children—including my mother—who had been fobbed off to orphanages and distant relations after that marriage dissolved.

Roy gave Betsy's children a sturdy home and a serenity they had never known up to then. They attended Catholic schools and ate with silverware and lap linens. My grandfather—black and white—and my grandmother—Chippewa Indian and white—reinvented themselves, creating new myths to cover their pasts and their olive skin.

They both knew their true heritage. My grandfather left Jim Crow Baton Rouge as a teenager, after all. My grandmother's mother was as red as the sunset. Nevertheless, they became paragons of clean white middle-class living. This was the 1950s. *Leave It to Beaver* was the top-rated show on television, and they did their best to live up to its example: a dining room decorated with priscilla curtains and crystal wineglasses.

Grandpa was known as "The Duke of Woodward Avenue" and left the post office to become the morning odds maker at the Detroit Race Course—a Teamsters track. He was good pals with Teamsters boss Jimmy Hoffa. My grandmother once showed me a photo of the two men holding picket signs in front of the track gates in the late sixties.

Their children tried to live up to the fancy white linen, but it was a little too late. They were too old to forget the pain of their scattered childhoods. Some got caught up in pregnancy, some with the law, some with alcohol.

Two years after his birth mother, Betty Zink, died alone in an upstairs apartment on the west side of Detroit, my father, Roy Jr., went off to the navy. And when Betsy Steele's daughter Evangeline came of age, she jumped on a train at the old Michigan Central Depot and met him in San Diego, where she became his wife.

She gave him a daughter, Nicole. Two months later, Roy Jr. shipped out as part of the first official U.S. combat troops in Vietnam.

When he returned, I was conceived.

So am I black? White? Mulatto? How much of anything am I? When I tried telling black people in Detroit my discovery, most would simply wave me off with a go-away-white-boy smirk. White folks laughed and called me Tyrone and asked if I was now ahead of them on the fire department hiring list.

In Detroit, I was reminded, old habits die hard.

Our family returned to Detroit in May 1967, just in time for the riots and the landing of the 82nd Airborne in the heart of the city to quell the violence.

It was a terribly muggy and uncomfortable evening when the fires started. My parents were living with my grandparents on the west side in the home built by the hands of my great-grandfather Henry, the sharecropper's son.

The riots officially started in the early hours of Sunday, July 23, when white cops began knocking black heads at an after-hours party. People started smashing things, but the real rampaging and looting did not begin until Sunday proper. The news media went out of its way to avoid reporting about the "disturbance," but the west side, where we lived, was already starting to burn. Even Willie Horton, the Tigers left fielder and a black man who had grown up near the ballpark, couldn't soothe the mob when he drove into the middle of it and stood on top of his car, still dressed

in his uniform from that afternoon's game. The city would burn for
five days.

My father was working that Sunday night at the old Wonder
Bread factory, which has since been replaced by the Motor City
Casino. My grandfather Roy, my grandmother Betsy and my mother,
Evangeline, holding me in her arms, stood on the front lawn around
dusk. The blacks were slowly moving out of their ghettos and setting up lives in the traditionally white areas of the city. If that weren't
bad enough, at least in my grandmother's mind, now the blacks
were burning the place down.

"Pa," she said to my grandfather, "we've got to get out of this
neighborhood."

To which my grandfather, a black man who never revealed the
fact to any of his relations, replied: "How many can there be?"

The following day, Grandpa got a gun.

JIHAD

AFTER MY AUNT'S FUNERAL, I dropped my wife and daughter at home and drove back to the paper. It was late afternoon. I was still dressed in my church clothes, including my fancy boots with the smooth, slippery lambskin soles.

The newsroom was a barnyard. Telephones were bleating. The flickering television sets were warbling. Reporters were cackling. This was the good part of newspapering. The Rush. This is what it sounds like when there is Breaking News.

The FBI had just raided a suburban warehouse and killed a man known as Imam Luqman Ameen Abdullah, the supreme and spiritual leader of a group of black Muslims who called themselves the Brotherhood.

The feds maintained that not only were Abdullah and his followers part of a radical Sunni jihadist organization intent on carving out an Islamic state within the United States through violent means, they were also fencing stolen fur coats and TV sets.

A sting to arrest Abdullah and his men was set up at a Dearborn warehouse about twenty miles west of downtown. The imam, a thin, bespectacled man who wore a cleaved goatee that made him look more like a circus clown than a conspiratorial mastermind, should have worn a Kevlar vest instead of the bulbous blue turban he fancied.

Because when agents instructed Abdullah and four underlings to put down their guns and put up their hands, the imam refused. A police dog was sent to flush him out of a semitrailer full of "stolen" flat-screen TVs that an undercover fed was selling to the imam to sell to other undercover feds.

This is when Abdullah is said to have fired on the police dog. The agents then fired on Abdullah, striking him twenty times.

The dog was rushed by helicopter for emergency surgery. The corpse of Abdullah was handcuffed and left on the floor of the semi-trailer until the medical examiner arrived. The dog died. An obituary appeared in the local papers. His named was Freddy. He was two years old.

The imam was taken to the Wayne County morgue. Dr. Schmidt, the medical examiner, told me later that he had never seen a corpse handcuffed the way the imam's was.

Jihadists. Fur coats. Blue turbans. Freddy the hero Belgian Malinois. I jumped in the *News'* car and raced to the Masjid Al-Haqq mosque on the west side of the city. The transmission whined: *Whirrr. Whirrr. Whirrr.*

I don't like to hit the ghetto in church clothes, especially in fancy boots with slippery lambskin soles, but things like militant black Muslims shooting it out with G-men comes around only so often for a newsman. And maybe this was the match that would start the Fourth Great Fire in Detroit.

I sparked a cigarette and stepped on it.

The mosque was located on Clairmount Street near Linwood, not far from the epicenter of the 1967 riot, not far from the apartment where my grandmother died alone a half century ago, not far from where my grandfather miraculously morphed from a black man into a white man.

The neighborhood looked like a photo from postwar Dresden. Row upon row of burnt-out houses, boarded storefronts, weedy and vacant lots peppered with shattered glass, sparkling like quartz tailings. The Soldier Boy meat market had long been dead. Joy Cleaners had run out of luck. The Rising Sun Grand Chapter of the O.E.S. fraternal organization had an unfriendly-looking bullet hole through its dirty window.

A bunch of tough-looking black men in robes and kaffiyeh scarves were milling around the mosque, which was no more than a crumbling house with a hand-painted sign that read in English and Arabic: THERE IS NO GOD BUT ALLAH.

"They bad dudes," a young woman whispered from her upper window, piecing together from my skin tone and notebook and lambskin boots that I must be a reporter. "They moved in about six months ago and took over the neighborhood. They just took over all them empty houses. Now our cars get stolen. They park on our grass, and you don't ask them to move. During Ramadan, they was sitting on them mosque steps smoking blunts and drinking Patrón and beer."

"I thought they were Muslims," I said.

"Muslims my ass," she snorted. "They's thugs."

I approached the crowd of robed men standing in front of the pillared porch, its roof sagging low. Four of them turned and started walking toward me. I hoped they noticed the notepad in my hand, the press card on a chain around my neck, the lambskin boots, my skin tone. Dressed in church clothes, I must have looked the very picture of a privileged professor of anthropology. Scenarios like this are the organ of adrenaline for a street reporter. This is why people cover war armed with only a pencil or a camera. Danger. My legs began to throb.

"Excuse me," I offered. "I'm sorry to hear about—"

"Nobody got nothing to say," the toughest-looking one said to me. His fists were balled. "We don't want none y'all coming round here. You hear?"

"I just—"

"Fuck off."

"Can I quote you on that?"

"I ain't gonna tell you again. Fuck off."

I fucked off.

I walked back to the weedy lot of glistening glass and stood smoking cigarettes with Brad Edwards, the hard-boiled newscaster from the Fox affiliate. As we smoked, Ricardo Thomas, a photographer from the *News*, drove up.

"You know where the mosque is?" Ricardo called from his window.

"Around the corner, man. Just look for the other photographers," I said. "But watch your ass, they're not in a happy mood."

Ricardo rolled his eyes. A sixty-seven-year-old black man, Ricardo had covered riots, murders and street protests in his long career. He knew the scene.

He drove off to get his photograph, and I forgot about him when Edwards struck up a conversation with a prostitute walking by.

"Y'all know what happened to them girls murdered on Gratiot?" she asked Edwards. She had bad teeth, good breasts and wore schoolteacher glasses.

"Were they working girls?" asked Edwards in his newsman's baritone. Edwards always seemed energized by a good murder story. "Someone's killing working girls? You know them?" He handed her his business card.

She took his card and smiled. Her teeth were ruined worse than the neighborhood. The sun was setting.

"No, I don't know them, but that's why I don't work past sunset," she said. "They crazy motherfuckers out here."

That's when the screaming started.

I spun around on my wooden heels. Ricardo was being pummeled by a dozen men from the mosque, enraged that he had taken photos after they warned him not to. Someone hit him with a wild haymaker and he fell, the back of his head bouncing off the curb. Someone snatched his cameras and whipped them repeatedly against the sidewalk.

I ran to him as best I could, slipping in my lamb-soled boots. In my mind—it all went in slow motion—I thought about it ending here, on a shitty corner in a desperate city. My last words would not be to my wife but to a twenty-dollar hooker with no dental insurance.

A mob is made up of men, and usually the men want to be stopped before they become a snarling pack. But there is a tipping point after which you can no longer stop them because "they" will have become an "it." I was hoping for my life and Ricardo's that the point hadn't been reached.

I approached from the back of the pack and grabbed Ricardo by his armpits and started skating backward. I was waiting for the glass bottle on the back of my head, but it never came. No one so much as touched me.

The men, realizing what they had done to an old man, shuffled shamefully back to their mosque; all except for the one carrying the broken cameras by their straps.

"Our leader was killed, man," he said with tears in his eyes as he walked away. "What the fuck's wrong with you?"

He was the guy who threatened me. I took it to be an apology. Ricardo didn't.

"I'm not afraid of you motherfuckers," he shouted.

The guy tossed the cameras in the gutter and walked away.

I noticed the sun had set.

"I was too cowardly to help," said an Associated Press man, walking up from the shadows with what was left of the cameras. It was a brave thing to admit. The cameras looked like battered cuckoo clocks.

Ricardo was giving his statement to the police when my cell phone rang. It was a cop source of mine. A high-up. I told him about Ricardo.

"Is he all right?" the voice asked with real concern.

"Yeah, I think so," I said.

"Do you have it on videotape?"

"Yeah, I think Fox got it," I said.

"Good," the cop said. "Send it to me. I love watching reporters get their ass kicked."

He said it deadpan.

"Listen," he went on. "You know Wyatt Earp Evans?"

He was talking about the new chief of police, Warren Evans, whose curious method of public relations was to ride along with his newly constituted "strike force" and bust down doors and snatch up guns.

"Well, you know how he likes to play big shot and go to see these shooting scenes?"

"Yeah?" I said. I had been out with him on one occasion. So had Edwards. So had ABC national news, for Christ's sake.

"Well," the cop said, "he got there a little too early tonight. His driver just put a cap in a kid."

"What?"

"Yep. Just shot a kid. Could you imagine if that was Bratton in L.A.?"

"International headlines," I said.

"Hell of a day in Detroit."

"You don't know the half of it," I said. "I'll call the news desk. Thanks."

I looked over. Ricardo was giving an interview to Edwards.

The shooting of a man in the presence of the chief of police earned nothing more than a three-paragraph story buried in the inside pages of the next morning's papers.

The FBI's shooting of the imam, however, was the stuff of international news, with lapdog headlines that could have been crafted by the FBI itself.

Detroit, according to media accounts, had a homegrown terror cell, and the feds had smashed it before it could wreak havoc on the populace.

It smelled like bullshit to me. What I saw at the mosque was a street gang, not a jihadist terror cell. In fact, reading over the charging documents presented to the federal judge that morning, the only conspiracy I could find was a clownish and amateur attempt by Abdullah and some of his henchmen to change the VIN plate on a stolen Ford Bronco. They had even given the truck the code name "White Lady."

These were not acolytes of Osama bin Laden. They were followers of H. Rap Brown, the former Black Panther and convert to Islam who was serving life in a Colorado supermax prison for killing a cop and wounding another in Georgia in 2000.

Part of the reason they were dealing in stolen goods, it seemed, was to get rent money for H. Rap's old lady in Atlanta.

The real acolyte of Osama bin Laden came to Detroit eight weeks later, on Christmas Day 2009, by airplane, with a bomb sewn into his underpants. In that case, the FBI and other federal agencies knew about Umar Farouk Abdulmutallab. They knew he supported jihad and knew he had met with senior al-Qaeda operatives and was planning something. Nevertheless, he was allowed to keep his U.S. visa and allowed to buy a plane ticket with cash. Flying from Amsterdam to Detroit on Northwest Airlines, Abdulmutallab lit his crotch bomb on fire above the city. Had the bomb not malfunctioned, it is possible that the airplane would have blown up. Had it blown up it is possible that it would have hit no one on the ground.

Detroit, by some estimates, is 40 percent vacant.

As for our jihadists, Abdullah and his men were caught on wire spinning fantasy scenarios about killing cops. But they never had a bomb and they never traveled to Yemen. They dealt in stolen property. They bullied neighbors and stole cars.

The Brotherhood was a gang, no doubt. But the FBI spin that this was a Sunni terror group was a silly overstatement. In fact, none of those arrested were charged with any terrorism counts, and a U.S. magistrate saw fit to release some of the eleven defendants on personal bond.

What I saw was a bunch of lost, pissed-off black men. Creatures of the ghetto—90 percent of whom had taken the well-worn path from the street block to the cell block and back to the corner, their lot never improving.

Imam Luqman Ameen Abdullah, a.k.a. Christopher Thomas, himself was introduced to Islam while in prison, and when he was released from incarceration, he began to create a Robin Hood thing in the ghetto. Carry guns. Rob to feed the poor. Espouse violence against the crown. Give yourself cool new names and costumes. Wear a turban. He gave lost men something to be and something to do.

But the fact is, he wasn't even a good thief. The Brotherhood was so broke, in fact, that the group was evicted from its previous mosque by the city for back taxes. What did the Brotherhood do? They simply walked a few blocks south and took over an abandoned house.

Frankly, the poverty is so severe in Detroit that I was surprised there weren't more groups like the Brotherhood bubbling up. Just a few weeks before Abdullah's killing, fifty thousand people had stormed Cobo Hall in hopes of getting one of the five thousand applications for federal rent and utilities assistance. The scene turned into a near riot, with people being trampled and applications being snatched from old people's hands.

"This morning, I seen the curtain pulled back on the misery," a man at Cobo told me. "People fighting over a line. People threatening to shoot each other. Is this what we've come to?"

Indeed.

Black nationalism is nothing new in Detroit. It is embroidered in the cultural quilt of the city. The Nation of Islam was founded here in the early 1930s by a mysterious figure named Wallace Fard Muhammad and taken to its apogee by Malcolm X, an ex-convict and Detroiter who preached emancipation "by any means necessary," only to be assassinated by his own. The Republic of New Afrika, a social movement that began in Detroit, espoused a separate black nation within the United States, to be carved out of the Deep South. Then there is the Shrine of the Black Madonna, the pan-African church from which the careers of Kwame Kilpatrick, Police Chief Evans and countless other political players in Detroit had sprung.

I had to get a look inside that mosque, and Kwame Kilpatrick gave me the key to the door.

Kilpatrick, in an effort to dodge his $6,000-a-month restitution payment to the city, had filed a motion claiming that when all of his living expenses in a posh Dallas suburb were deducted from his salesman's check, he had only $6 a month left.

The prosecutor—pissed off with the game and seeking to revoke Kilpatrick's probation and toss him into state prison—hauled the former mayor into court the morning after the imam was shot.

The prosecutor pulled back the curtain on Kilpatrick's lavish lifestyle: Gucci shoes, nail salons, plastic surgery for his wife, a million-dollar house and private school for the kids. Under oath, Kilpatrick claimed he didn't know what his wife did for a living because she had him living in the basement in their rich, white Texas neighborhood.

When asked by the prosecutor what exactly he had spent a half million dollars on over the last year, Kilpatrick invoked his Fifth Amendment privilege—three separate times. That's one thing the ex-mayor, the hit man and I have in common. We know our constitutional law.

Then came the detail that gave me the key to the mosque door. The prosecutor exposed the fact that a group of white suburban businessmen had given Kilpatrick and his wife nearly $300,000 in parting gifts and loans when he was forced out of city hall.

These self-made businessmen—Peter Karmanos, Dan Gilbert, Roger Penske, James Nicholson and Matty Moroun—still realized there was plenty of loot to be made in a dead city. They were some of the same men who bundled together the last-minute cash in 2005 that saved Kilpatrick's struggling reelection campaign. What these white men got in return for their charity was anybody's guess. But for a fleeting moment, Detroiters got a taste of the vanilla icing that coats Chocolate City.

I went back to the mosque the following morning with the newspaper. It was Friday, the Muslim Sabbath. The Brotherhood, I knew, would all be gathering for prayers.

I showed the Kilpatrick headline to a man named Jamel, a security guard who was smoking a cigarette out front on the porch. He looked at me with a tired skepticism before scanning the article. I noticed the irises of his eyes were ringed in blue.

"The white man finds a monkey and dresses up the monkey in a suit," Jamel sneered, handing me back the paper. "The monkey does the white man's bidding and makes himself rich. Then the monkey's talking shit about the white man. Games. And the people's out here suffering. What do you think we been trying to say?"

A man lighter than an Irish grandmother and dressed in a cotton gown started an argument with Jamel for speaking with me, "Whitey."

It was turning loud and ugly, and remembering Ricardo, I was heading for my car when Omar Regan, one of Imam Abdullah's twelve children, arrived and calmed everyone down with a simple "Brothers." He invited me upstairs for prayers.

Taking his cue, the Irishman bowed and took my hand while

introducing himself by his Muslim name, taken straight from CNN: Jihad al Jihad.

Regan is a young, handsome, powerful orator who speaks Arabic and leads a mosque in South Central Los Angeles. He had come for his father's funeral and had washed his father's body and anointed his feet with oil the evening before. He told me his father had been shot twenty times, once through the scrotum.

The crowd was overflowing and the sermon was broadcast onto the street. Inside, the mosque had exposed walls and electrical boxes with no switches. The malfunctioning furnace gave off an oppressive heat, made worse by the pressed-together bodies.

"How can you be what they say you are, when you don't got nothing," Regan preached to the weeping congregants. "They forgot about the 'hood. The suburbs are okay, but they forgot about the 'hood. They forgot about you, and so we all, my Muslim brothers, have to take care of each other.

"They call us radicals. They call us terrorists. We don't care what they say about us because they don't care about what's good."

The killing of Abdullah had only made things worse, I could see. And as I sat there scribbling in my notebook, I wondered why the federal agents couldn't simply have arrested the imam while he went to get a morning cup of coffee.

As I looked up, two people stood to accept conversion to Islam.

WHITE MAN'S BURDEN

IT WAS A beautiful December morning in southern California. The 405 freeway was bumper to bumper, which was either a good or bad sign for the American car industry, depending on how one looked at it—good because Americans were clearly still buying cars, bad because half of them appeared to be foreign brands.

It was the morning before the Los Angeles Auto Show officially kicked off, and Cadillac was holding a reporters-only preview of the CTS Coupe, the newest member of the Cadillac family, set to hit showrooms in 2010. The new car was being touted as one of the models that would bring General Motors back to profitability, allowing it to pay off its astronomical debt to the American taxpayer.

The company had rented out an off-site dance studio and placed five silver Cadillacs on the open dance floor. Cloth-covered tables lined the entrance, and smartly dressed waiters brought lunch to reporters as they looked over the vehicles.

Back in Detroit, something was brewing. GM announced it

would be holding a press conference at 4:30 P.M. But the news leaked early.

As the reporters in L.A. sipped ice tea and nibbled on rubbery salmon, a GM beat writer held up his BlackBerry: "Fritz Henderson, GM CEO, resigns."

Henderson was the GM insider who took over as CEO after Rick Wagoner was forced out by Obama. Now Henderson was being forced out and replaced by Edward Whitacre, the administration's handpicked chairman of the GM board, who would take on both jobs.

The reporter with the BlackBerry looked over at one of Cadillac's global marketing men and asked, "Do you have any reaction to Fritz Henderson's resignation?"

"What?" The marketing man choked, freezing in his chair.

The reporter repeated the question, holding out his BlackBerry. "Fritz just resigned."

"Holy shit," gulped the marketing man.

And then the dance studio became the set of a bad movie. All around, reporters were clicking away at their smart phones. GM executives and others were scurrying back and forth, murmuring and mumbling and stumbling.

As reporters ran to the door to fetch their cars from the valet, another public relations man from Cadillac was standing near the entrance, cursing.

"Fuck, fuck, fuck, fuck. Why the fuck would Fritz Henderson do this today, the day before the L.A. show? All of those stories everyone was going to write about the CTS Coupe are gone, they're walking out the door right now."

He was right. Even the *Detroit News* wasn't going to mention the new Caddy. The Henderson firing was huge news. Seemed like little had changed in the executive offices back in Detroit. They still hadn't gotten their shit together.

Meanwhile, the Cadillac executives in Los Angeles gathered in a single office to take a conference call from Detroit. They were obviously being told what had transpired in the Renaissance Center. The only problem was that the office was glass, and the remaining reporters just stood outside of it and watched the hand-wringing. You could see the shock in their slumped shoulders and exasperated expressions.

Who the fuck was running the country?

Later that night, well past deadline, reporters were drinking in the hotel bar, trying to clear their heads for the morning go-around before going to bed.

A GM executive was there, easily ten drinks into the evening, judging by the smell of gin and olives on his breath.

"The new board of directors are fucking crazy," he slurred. "Every time they meet, someone gets fired. Every thirty days, we're scared shitless because they don't have any idea how a car company works."

He went on, telling how the board kept asking executives to produce a hybrid—something that can't be done in thirty days—and about other unattainable, if not impossible, demands from Washington.

The executive's voice cracked with desperation and alcohol, the burden of the day's failure weighing heavy on him.

"Worse yet, Fritz resigns today. Why would you let him quit the day before four of your most important vehicles are set to debut? The Buick Regal, the Chevy Cruze, the Cadillac CTS Coupe and the Chevy Volt? Are they trying to ruin us?"

Here was a man who loved GM, loved it more than any reporter ever could, and he was watching the company as he knew it disintegrate before his eyes. He believed that there was a conspiracy to undermine all of the GM execs.

The Fritz Henderson "resignation" didn't surprise many people; he was a lame duck at best, but the timing couldn't have been worse, and everybody already knew that what the executive was saying was true. Detroit may be a hidebound and inept culture allergic to change, but so too is Washington. Auto insiders sitting at the bar stirring their olives wondered how long this arranged marriage could last. No one in Detroit was going to care about the L.A. Auto Show. Not the editors, not the readers and not anyone else in the world. It was a colossal clusterfuck.

The next morning, as reporters entered the Los Angeles Convention Center, there was a sign announcing that Bob Lutz, GM's vice chairman, would be giving the keynote address during the breakfast instead of Henderson, who was the originally scheduled speaker.

Lutz's name was written on white tape and placed over Henderson's on the signboard pointing to the room where the speech would be given.

But like a bad painting, you could still read Henderson's name underneath.

FEAR NO EVIL

THE VOICE OF the old woman was threadbare and sad.

"I need a few hundred dollars," Big Martha asked me meekly. "I'm haunted by that closet. Every time I walk by it now, I get so sad. It don't seem right that Little Martha should spend a second Christmas up in there. It ain't really for Martha I'm asking. She's gone on. Murder always stays murder forever, I suppose. I'm asking the favor for myself."

I felt that I had unleashed some terrible emotions that Big Martha had stuffed away deep in a pantry when I had come knocking a few weeks earlier, and I felt obligated to fix things. I wanted to make things right for her. For Christmas. I made some calls.

When I explained the situation to the manager of the Sacred Heart Cemetery, he promised to provide a plot for Little Martha on top of her grandfather for $450. A stonecutter said he would supply a simple marble marker with the names of both Martha Anne and her grandfather, Clarence, for $199.

I didn't have the heart to tell Big Martha that a Polish man was buried beneath Clarence in what is called a double plot. But I put the detail in a small newspaper story that got picked up by Angelo Henderson, a former newspaperman who found better fortune in the pulpit of talk radio.

Detroit is full of good people who know what pain is, and they sent more than $3,000 by mail, some in tens, some in fifties, the extra money going to a soup kitchen of Big Martha's choice. One man even gave Big Martha the money for the car she needed. If there is any hope for Detroit it is the thousands of good people like this, afraid but not wanting to be afraid anymore.

It was cold and overcast in the morning, the snow falling like a shower of needles. I picked up Big Martha in the *News* car. *Whirrr. Whirrr. Whirrr.*

She clutched the urn containing Little Martha to her bosom. Little Martha's mother, Sharon, was too busy with her demons and cigarettes to leave the musty little house.

"I don't know what's wrong with them people" was all Big Martha said about her family—none were coming to the graveyard. She was silent the rest of the way to the funeral.

When we arrived, the cemetery manager was waiting with a shovel, the stonecutter with the headstone. The manager then turned over a little dirt on top of the grave that Big Martha's husband shared with the unknown Pole who lay below him.

We buried Little Martha's ashes. Big Martha forgot her Bible, so I read Psalm 23 from an iPhone, but Big Martha cried anyway, shivering in her thin shoes.

Yea, though I walk through the valley of the shadow of death, I will fear no evil, for thou art with me.

She hugged the stonecutter and I drove her home.

We got lost in her neighborhood, since Big Martha doesn't get around much except to walk to church or the bus stop.

"You know something, Mr. Charlie?"

"Charlie."

"You know something, Charlie? I knew you was coming. I knew it because before you did, I put my last forty dollars in the collection plate and prayed. Now the Lord says, 'Giveth and ye shall receive tenfold.'"

"And the preacher shall receiveth a new Cadillac," I said.

She laughed. "You right about that."

"Now don't go giving him your new-car money, Martha. That's for your car, not the reverend's."

"My Lord," she said, studying the boulevard. "Look at all these churches. How can there be so many churches? Who goes to 'em all?"

"I've wondered that myself."

"We ought to do it like white people," Martha said. "Just have two or three different kinds of churches. All these churches we black folks have don't seem to be accomplishing much."

Finding her street, I pulled up to the little HUD house that the city in its wisdom would soon be taking away from her.

"Merry Christmas, Martha."

"Thank you, Charlie. Thank you. May the Lord shine on you."

Murder Always Stays
Murder Forever

WE HAD GOTTEN one innocent lamb a proper and decent burial. Now I had to make sure we didn't have to bury a jackass.

I remembered the conversation I had with the hit man while standing in my underwear. He had threatened to wipe out a prosecutor for making his identity as a snitch known to the dope crew he ran with.

I called the assistant prosecutor and told him about the hit man's threats. I didn't call because I liked him. I thought the prosecutor was a weasel. A tight-assed bureaucrat who was more concerned with closing a case than getting justice.

In the end I didn't call him out of any moral or journalistic obligation. I figured it was probably illegal not to tell a prosecutor that someone was looking to ice him.

So I called.

"Tell me exactly what he said about me. Did he threaten to kill me?"

"Well, I'm not sure," I said, starting to regret the call. "Not exactly. It was implied, maybe."

"Did he or didn't he?" the prosecutor said in a pinched-nose tone.

"Why are you asking?"

"Because we'll have to pick him up."

"On what grounds?" I asked.

"For threatening a prosecutor."

"Wait a minute!" I screamed. "I'm calling you as a gentleman. You're going to arrest a killer on the grounds that I told you he was upset with you? What's to stop him from coming after me?"

The prosecutor, who had been known to wear a bulletproof vest beneath his Oxford shirt while in court, squealed, "I'm not going to get shot by [the informant]!

"Hold on a moment," he fumbled. "I want you to tell that to my supervisor. Tell it exactly as you told it to me to my supervisor."

"I can't tell you any more," I said. "You do what you got to do."

I hung up the phone.

That weekend, I moved my family out of the house.

If a suburban prosecutor and a suburban reporter fear for their lives, imagine what it's like to live in the rough Detroit neighborhoods.

Sumayah Tauheed closed the barbershop where Alexander and Alls worked two days after Alls was assassinated. She thought she was next.

Tauheed agreed to meet me at the shop, about a quarter mile from the Detroit Police Central Precinct.

When I arrived, she insisted that the door be padlocked from the inside.

"Is that really necessary?" I asked. "It's broad daylight."

"Trust me," she said. Then the forty-seven-year-old grand-mother lifted her purse. She had a .38 strapped to her waistline.

"I just got it," she said. "At least I got a fifty-fifty chance."

It was the first Monday of the month: Social Security check day.

At the very moment Tauheed was showing me her piece—outside the door, just feet from where Alls was murdered—an old man was being bludgeoned across the face. Two young men had tailed him from a check-cashing joint. They savaged him and robbed him of $500. They broke his two front teeth.

We fumbled with the padlock trying to get out to help, but by the time we got the door open, the muggers were long gone down the street. There was nothing but a bloody old man and an aban-doned mattress.

The ambulance arrived. Eventually, the police came too.

"It's despicable," said a white cop with Roy Orbison glasses. "Watch your ass around here."

Tauheed and I watched him drive off.

"The police don't run the streets," she said. "The gangs run the streets."

There's not much a newspaper reporter can do about dead men. But a newspaper reporter and a cop and a judge can deliver some justice. That's why the founding fathers wrote it up the way they did, I sup-pose. Life. Liberty. Pursuit of happiness. Everyone is entitled to those things. My news story about the hit man and Little Martha and the trail of bodies following Deandre Woolfolk hit the streets the morn-ing of the preliminary trial—a hearing to determine if there was enough evidence to bind the defendants Woolfolk, Johnson and Cooley over for the nightclub beating death.

And of course there wasn't enough evidence. The only witness had been murdered. But everyone involved that morning had read the story of Alls, the wannabe cop, getting rubbed out because he had the guts to stand up and testify as a witness to a beating death.

They read about Little Martha. They read her last words: "What's happening?" They read about her spending eternity in a linen closet.

They read about Woolfolk being kicked free from jail even though he admitted to chipping in on the girl's murder.

They read about the hit man, his protestations and his threats to kill the prosecutor.

They read about the frustrated cop who'd filled me in on this whole steaming shit pile.

They read about the bodies.

I sat in the jury box and smiled as the lawyers and the weak-kneed prosecutor bitterly complained that the case had been leaked to the media.

The attorney for Woolfolk—the killer of Little Martha—pointed at me in the jury box, complaining that I had poisoned his client's ability to get a fair hearing.

"I didn't say anything to the reporter," the prosecutor said with a shrug.

Then Sgt. Mike Martel was called to the stand. Woolfolk's attorney adjusted his plaid suit coat. It hung on him as though it were trying to crawl away.

The guy fancied himself a regional Johnnie Cochran. And he may have dressed like Cochran, but he possessed none of Cochran's cunning. He addressed Sergeant Martel, who was sworn in and sitting in the witness chair.

"The judge told you in this case not to release information with respect to tapes and identification of parties; you did that anyhow, didn't you, sir?"

Martel sat up in the witness box and rubbed his knuckles. "I wasn't advised by this court to do or not do anything," he said.

"Did you give the [hit man] the news reporter's number?"

The lawyer looked over at me. I gave a little wave. He turned back to Martel, who did not acknowledge me.

"I discussed it with the witness."

"Were you the person that showed the news reporter the tape, sir?"

"Yes."

"Okay. Were you the person who felt confident that by showing the news reporter the tape that you would be furthering justice?"

"It had nothing to do with justice," Martel said.

"Basically, you were mad at the prosecutor and therefore you were going to get out information you wanted to get out to the public?"

"It had to do with exposing conduct."

"Are you talking about the judge now or the prosecutor?"

"The prosecutor."

"Oh!" shouted the lawyer, theatrically peeling his glasses from his face. "You wanted to go after the prosecutor! Is that it?"

"I didn't go after anybody," Martel said coolly.

"You vilified the prosecutor because he didn't follow your suggestion as to how he ran the case! I have nothing further."

He sat down. His jacket shoulders stayed up, and Martel left the courtroom with his broad chin high.

Later that afternoon, Martel called me: "How did I do?"

"Unbelievable," I said. "You got a set on you." I had never seen a cop admit that he'd leaked sensitive information to a reporter. Especially in court.

"I'm not going to lie," he answered.

The judge was a cautious one. And the preliminary trial dragged on for weeks. During that time I was supplied by the police a videotape of a strip-club shoot-up. It showed Eiland Johnson—one of the codefendants—walking into the club dressed in shorts and a tank top and opening up with a semiautomatic pistol before running out. I was struck by one hero in the lower right frame of the videotape, a big guy who shielded himself by grabbing a stripper and throwing her toward the gunman. I began my newspaper story this way:

> DETROIT—According to police accounts, not only does Eiland Johnson not know how to behave at a nightclub, he doesn't know how to dress for one either.

As I sat in the gallery waiting for court to begin, a young black woman leaned into me. She wore a long black wig, long purple nails and a set of outrageous eyelashes that looked like fans made of plucked chicken feathers. Her breasts were spilling out of her blouse. Her lips were full and ravenous and moist and it looked as though she could suck the snout of a hog clean with those things. She was a girlfriend of Woolfolk's and kept tilting her tits so he could get a nice long look. He licked his lips as though he were staring into a plate of stuffed chops. The fact that he was facing life in prison did not register. This seemed more like an early morning field trip.

"'Scuse me," his woman whispered to me. "Are you that man who wrote the story that Eiland don't know how to dress?"

"Yeah, that was me," I said, nervous that Woolfolk's crew knew me by sight.

"That was hilarious," Little Miss Piggy said, touching my forearm. "We was all passing that story around. He don't know how to dress. You funny."

"Thank you," I said, relieved, thinking that the boss would be pleased to learn that I had expanded our ever-shrinking readership in the community—to a group of young urban residents with disposable incomes, no less.

The star witness, the hit man who had called me threatening to kill the prosecutor, was supposed to testify.

Except the hit man sat cowering in the holding cell behind the courtroom, invoking his Fifth Amendment right not to incriminate himself. The prosecutor was hoping the hit man would tell the judge that Alls had been ordered dead. If the judge believed it, she might allow Alls's statements to police to be entered into evidence: that Alls saw these men beat his best friend to death with liquor bottles and a rope stanchion in the middle of a packed nightclub, all because someone groped a woman's ass.

But the hit man knew what Big Martha and everyone else in Detroit knew: *a murder always stays murder, forever.*

"Let's take ten minutes," ordered Susan Moiseev, whose title, according to the lettering affixed to the bench below her, was DISTRI T JUDGE. The *C* had fallen off long ago.

I wandered about the hallway and examined the photos of the district judges pinned to a corkboard behind locked glass panels. The photos were old and fading, stained with red and yellow blotches from where sunlight had interacted with the chemicals. I tried the water fountain. It trickled like stale mud. There was no noise. The place had the lonesome whiff of decay. A suburban courthouse built long ago to fulfill the promises the city couldn't deliver—only to find that suburban justice couldn't deliver the promise either.

I stood and watched the girlfriends and mothers of the defendants whisper in a corner near the window.

Back in the courtroom, the lawyer for Cooley, the boss of the Black Mafia Family, made a convincing argument.

"Your honor," said Steve Fishman, "if my client, Mr. Cooley, sells dope all around the United States, what's that have to do with the murder of an individual? Did Darnell Cooley have something to do with keeping Anthony Alls from testifying? I don't have to submit any evidence that Mr. Cooley had nothing to do with Alls's murder.

"It doesn't matter if he sold mounds of cocaine. There is no evidence to connect him to it."

Judge Moiseev was unmoved. She allowed Alls's statements to be entered as evidence and bound the three over for trial.

The defendants frowned. Before deputies dragged them back to jail with their hands manacled, Woolfolk leaned toward Little Miss Piggy with her moist mouth and poked out his nose toward her tits as though sniffing for a bouquet of lilacs. Little Miss Piggy tilted toward him and smiled like a wet nurse.

Fishman, who also represented Monica Conyers in her federal bribery case, is a very good lawyer. It's said about him that he'd win more cases if he actually represented more innocent people.

Unperturbed, Fishman buckled up his briefcase and left.

When the courtroom cleared, I approached the judge.

"That was ballsy of you," I said to her. "There's not a whole lot of evidence."

"Your article put a lot of pressure on everybody," she said. "Let the next judge deal with it. I'm not running for reelection.

"Besides," she said of Woolfolk, "bodies seem to follow that guy wherever he goes."

How right she was. A few months later, the estranged wife of the unwilling hit man received a text message from his phone: "Your boy is dead," it read.

Somebody whacked the hit man. His body has never been found.

But Sergeant Martel had a second theory. "He might've sent the text himself in an effort to avoid child-support payments. We ain't dealing with St. Joseph here."

As for the three members of the Black Mafia Family—they all took a deal for three to five years in prison.

Not much, but better than nothing.

FORGET WHAT YOU SAW

IT WAS JUST after midnight and the streetlights were out on Lillibridge Street. It is like that all over Detroit, where whole blocks regularly go dark with no warning or any apparent pattern. Inside the lower unit of a duplex halfway down the gloomy street, Charles Jones was pacing, unable to sleep, something on his mind.

His seven-year-old daughter, Aiyana Mo'nay Stanley-Jones, slept on the couch as her grandmother watched television. Outside, television was watching them. A half dozen masked officers of the Special Response Team—Detroit's version of SWAT—were at the door, guns drawn.

The SWAT team tried the steel door to the building. It was unlocked. They threw a flash-bang grenade through the window of the lower unit and kicked open its wooden door, which was also unlocked. The grenade landed so close to Aiyana that it burned her blanket. Officer Joseph Weekley, the lead commando, fired a single shot, the bullet striking Aiyana in the head and exiting her neck. It all happened in a matter of seconds.

"They had time," Mike Carlisle told me when I called him. He was waiting at the airport to chauffeur some Italian auto executive to the Chrysler headquarters. "You don't go into a home around midnight. People are drinking. People are awake. Me? I would have waited until the morning when the guy went to the liquor store to buy a quart of milk. That's how it's supposed to be done."

But the SWAT team didn't wait. Maybe because the cameras were rolling, maybe because a Detroit police officer had been murdered two weeks earlier while trying to apprehend a suspect. This was the first raid on a house since his death.

Police first floated the story that Aiyana's grandmother had grabbed Weekley's gun. Then, realizing that sounded like bullshit, they said she'd brushed the gun as she ran past the door. But the grandmother said she was lying on the far side of the couch, away from the door. Plus, grenades are rarely used when rounding up suspects, even murder suspects. But it was dark. And TV may have needed some pyrotechnics.

"It was a total fuckup," a police commander in charge of this total fuckup told me the next morning. "A total, unfortunate fuckup."

In tow was an A&E crew filming an episode of *The First 48*, its true-crime program. The conceit of the show is that homicide detectives have forty-eight hours to crack a murder case before the trail goes cold. Thirty-four hours earlier, Je'Rean Blake Nobles, seventeen, had been shot outside a liquor store on nearby Mack Avenue; an informant had ID'd a man named Chauncey Owens as the shooter and provided this address.

Compounding the tragedy is the fact that the police threw the grenade into the wrong apartment. Chauncey Owens lived in the upstairs flat with Charles Jones's sister.

Owens, a habitual criminal, was arrested upstairs minutes after

Aiyana's shooting and charged with the slaying of Je'Rean. His motive, authorities say, was that the teen failed to pay him the proper respect. And Jones—the father of the slain little girl—was later charged with Je'Rean's murder too; he allegedly went along for the ride.

As Officer Weekley wept on the sidewalk, his colleagues trying to console him over his wayward shot, Aiyana was rushed to the trauma table, where she was pronounced dead. Her body was transferred to the Wayne County morgue and Dr. Schmidt.

I went to visit the doctor. A Hollywood starlet was tailing him, studying for her role as the medical examiner in ABC's new Detroit-based murder drama *Detroit 1-8-7*. The title is derived from the California penal code for murder: 187. In Michigan, the designation for homicide is actually 750.316, but that's just a mouthful of detail.

The starlet giggled as she sliced up a dead man's brain.

"You might say that the homicide of Aiyana is the natural conclusion to the disease from which she suffered," Schmidt told me.

"What disease was that?" I asked.

"The psychopathology of growing up in Detroit," he said. "Some people are doomed from birth because their environment is so toxic."

When I was a teenager, my mother and I were working in her little flower shop not far from where Aiyana would be killed. It was a hot afternoon around Mother's Day and I walked across the street to the liquor store for a soda pop. A small crowd of agitated black people was gathered on the sidewalk. The store bell jingled its little requiem as I pulled the door open.

Inside, splayed on the floor underneath the rack of snack cakes near the register, was a black man in a pool of blood. The blood was congealing into a pancake on the dirty linoleum. His eyes and mouth were open and held that milky expression of a drunk who has fallen asleep with his eyes open. The red halo around his skull gave the scene a feeling of serenity.

An Arab family owned the store, and one of the men—the one with the pocked face and loud voice—was talking on the telephone, but I remember no sounds. His brother stood over the dead man, a pistol in his hand, keeping an eye on the door in case someone walked in wanting to settle things.

"You should go," he said to me, shattering the silence with a wave of his hand. "Forget what you saw, little man. Go." He wore a gold bracelet as thick as a gymnasium rope. I lingered a moment, backing out while taking it in: the bracelet, the liquor, the blood, the gun, the Ho Hos, the cheapness of it all.

The flower shop is just a pile of bricks now, but despite what the Arab told me, I did not forget what I saw. Whenever I see a person who died of violence or misadventure, I think about the dead man with the open eyes on the dirty floor of the liquor store. I've seen him in the faces of soldiers when I was covering the Iraq War. I saw him in the face of my sister. I saw him in the face of my sister's daughter. And I saw him now, on the face of a willowy child in a casket. Another innocent, whose death triggered a series of events that almost set the ghetto on fire.

Je'Rean Blake Nobles was one of the rare black males in Detroit who made it through high school. A good kid with average grades, Je'Rean went to Southeastern High, which is situated in an industrial belt of moldering Chrysler assembly plants. Completed in 1917, the school, attended by white students at the time, was considered so far out in the wilds that its athletic teams took the nickname "Jungaleers."

With large swaths of the city now rewilding—empty lots are returning to prairie and woodland as the city depopulates—Southeastern was slated to absorb students from nearby Kettering High as part of a massive school-consolidation effort. That is, until someone realized that the schools are controlled by rival gangs. So bad is the rivalry that when the schools face off to play football or basketball, spectators from the visiting team are banned.

Southeastern's motto is *Age Quod Agis*: "Attend to Your Business." And Je'Rean did. By wit and will, he managed to make it through. A member of JROTC, he was on his way to the military recruitment office after senior prom and commencement. But Je'Rean never went to the prom, much less the Afghanistan theater, because he couldn't clear the killing fields of Detroit. He became a horrifying statistic—in Detroit more than five children are murdered every month.

Je'Rean's crime? He looked at Chauncey Owens the wrong way.

It was 2:40 in the afternoon when Je'Rean went to the Motor City liquor store and ice cream stand to get himself an orange juice to wash down his McDonald's. About forty kids were milling around in front of the soft-serve window. That's when Owens, thirty-four, pulled up on a moped.

Je'Rean might have thought it was funny to see a grown man driving a moped. He might have smirked. But he said nothing.

"Why you looking at me?" said Owens, getting off the moped. "Do you got a problem or something? What the fuck you looking at?"

A slender, pimply-faced kid, Je'Rean was not an intimidating figure. One witness had him pegged for thirteen years old.

Je'Rean balled up his tiny fist. "What?" he croaked.

"Oh, stay your ass right here," Owens growled. "I got something for you."

Owens sped two blocks back to Lillibridge and gathered up a posse, according to his own statement to the police. The posse allegedly included Aiyana's father, Charles "C.J." Jones.

"It's some lil niggas at the store talking shit—let's go whip they ass," Owens told his crew of grown men.

Owens switched his moped for a Chevy Blazer. Jones and two other men known as "Lil' James" and "Dirt" rode along for Je'Rean's ass-whipping. Lil' James brought along a .357 Magnum—at the behest of Jones, because Jones was afraid someone would try to steal his "diamond Cartier glasses."

Je'Rean knew badness was on its way and called his mother to come pick him up. She arrived too late. Owens got there first and shot Je'Rean clear through the chest with Lil' James's gun. Clutching his juice in one hand and two dollars in the other, Je'Rean staggered across Mack Avenue and collapsed in the street. A minute later, a friend took the two dollars as a keepsake. A few minutes after that, Je'Rean's mother, Lyvonne Cargill, arrived and got behind the wheel of the car that friends had dragged him into.

Why would anyone move a gunshot victim, much less toss him in a car? It is a matter of conditioning. In Detroit, the official response time of an ambulance to a 911 call is twelve minutes. Paramedics say it is routinely twice that. Sometimes they come in a Crown Victoria with only a defibrillator and a blanket, because there are no other units available.

The hospital was six miles away. Je'Rean's mother drove as he gurgled in the backseat.

"My baby, my baby, my baby. God, don't take my baby."

They made it to the trauma ward, where Je'Rean was pronounced dead. His body was transferred to Dr. Schmidt and the Wayne County morgue.

Rocket Docket

THE RAID ON the Lillibridge house that took little Aiyana's life came two weeks and at least a dozen homicides after the last time police stormed into a Detroit home. That house too is on the city's east side, a nondescript brick duplex with a crumbling garage whose driveway funnels into busy Schoenherr Road.

Responding to a breaking-and-entering and shots-fired call at 3:30 A.M., Officer Brian Huff, a twelve-year veteran, walked into that dark house. Behind him stood two rookies. His partner took the rear entrance. Huff and his partner were not actually called to the scene; they'd taken it upon themselves to assist the younger cops, according to the police version of events.

Huff entered with his gun still holstered. Behind the door was Jason Gibson, a violent man with a history of gun crimes, assaults on police, and repeated failures to honor probationary sentences. Even so, the judges continued to revolving-door him back onto the streets, because the overwhelmed jails and courts could barely process the murderers and rapists and politicians. This often leads to murder.

Gibson was a tall, thick-necked man who, like the television character Omar from *The Wire*, made his living robbing dope houses. Which is what he was doing at this house, authorities contend, when he put three bullets in Officer Huff's face, killing him.

A neighbor who now tends the lawn of the abandoned dope house out of respect for Huff wondered why so many cops had even showed up to the routine home-invasion call. "The police hardly come around at all, much less that many cops that fast on a break-in."

Some newspapermen I worked with believed Huff may have been running a dope house in the duplex. That was the word their sources were giving them. Like the neighbor now tending the lawn, reporters and cops alike wondered why Huff and a half dozen cops rushed to a run-of-the-mill call that wasn't even assigned to them by the dispatcher.

I couldn't have cared less why they all showed up that evening. I was more interested in the fact that once Huff went down and the gunfire went off, it was the cops who shot each other.

But the biggest mystery behind Officer Huff's murder is why Gibson was out on the street in the first place. A few years earlier, Gibson attacked a cop and tried to take his gun. For that he was given simple probation. And he failed to report to court.

Why would a menace who tried to disarm a cop be given probation? The answer is as sad as it is simple. The Detroit jails and the courts are administered by Wayne County, and the county government is as corrupt and mismanaged as the city's.

The standard reason for men like Gibson getting probation is that there aren't enough jail beds. But the truth is, half the jail beds sit empty because there is no money to pay deputies to guard the inmates.

In order to relieve this "overcrowding" in the jails and courtrooms, something known as the "rocket docket" was concocted. Put simply: if someone is not accused of a capital crime like murder or rape, they are funneled through the court's rocket docket at light speed and generally given probation or an electronic monitoring anklet. Too many times, dangerous men escape into the ether, which Gibson did.

Police caught him again, a year before he killed Huff. That time, he was in possession of a handgun stolen from an Ohio cop.

Again Gibson went through the rocket docket and was set free on $2,000 bond in January. Incredibly, he showed up for his trial in circuit court in February.

But then the circuit court too has its gangrenous limbs in need of pruning. His judge, Cynthia Gray Hathaway, adjourned the trial without explanation, according to official paperwork. Known as "Half-Day" Hathaway, she was part of an extended clan of judges related by blood and marriage who held great power over the halls of justice. And because judges are elected in Michigan, name recognition means everything and legal ability almost nothing. For this reason you could find Hathaways rooted on the benches from family court to the Michigan Supreme Court.

Judge Cynthia Gray Hathaway was removed from the bench for six months by the Michigan Supreme Court a decade earlier for, among other things, adjourning trials to sneak away on vacation.

After his adjournment by Hathaway, Gibson did not show for his new court date.

I got a call from a high-ranking prosecutor.

"Dude, come meet me. You're not going to believe what I found."

We met at a coffee shop in midtown. He was wearing suspenders and a sour face. I took a seat and he tossed a manila folder at my elbows.

"Take a look," he said.

The day after Huff was killed, and under fire from the police for her leniency toward Gibson, Judge Hathaway went into the case file and made changes, according to notations made in the court's computerized docket system.

"Holy shit," I said.

"She fucking killed that cop," he said. "She had to know Gibson was going to run. That's all he ever did."

"What did she change?" I asked.

"I don't know. Go to her courtroom. Ask for the case file. It's public record."

We shook hands.

I went to the judge's courtroom. Not only would she not come out from behind the oak doors, she refused to let me see the original paper file, despite the fact that it is a public record. Her clerk said the judge could not comment on the case because she might preside in the trial against Gibson.

I went back to the office and wrote it up with my colleague who covered courts for the *News*. Inexplicably, our report sat for days. And when it did appear in the paper the next week, it was watered down to the point of being a half story. Explanations were made on the judge's behalf, but not by the judge herself. Instead, we took the word of her supervisor that everything was on the up and up.

Editorial decisions like this are made all the time in the news business. But the changes in the copy were never checked with me, as is the custom. When I went to the editors for an explanation, I was told "there were questions" with the original copy.

I've been in the business long enough to translate what that meant: we don't want to piss off a judge unless we're absolutely sure.

As right as the editors may have been, I was done. Maybe we couldn't clean up Detroit, but here we had a lazy judge running for reelection and we could have at least done something about that. How long were we going to slog through this river of shit pretending?

I called my buddy the janitor and had him bring a trash can on wheels up to the newsroom. When he did, I swept the entire contents of my desktop into the garbage and walked out.

On my way to the stairs, I looked up at the bank of television sets where I had seen the story of Kilpatrick and the dead stripper on my first day of work nearly two years earlier.

The screens had gone dark.

Outside, I stopped and lit a cigarette and leaned against the building. I thought about what I had just done. I had turned my back on the newspaper business and I was sad. I love being a newsman and I believe in the words carved in the sandstone parapet of the *News* building: TROUBLER OF THE PUBLIC CONSCIENCE.

But that ideal had become as ossified as the statue of Benjamin Franklin up there. From New York to Los Angeles, American newspapers were yellow and stale before they even came off the press. Dog beaten by a dwindling readership, financial losses and partisan attacks, editors had stripped them of their personality in an attempt to offend no one. And so there was no more reason to read them. Safety before Truth. Grammar over Guts. Winners before Losers. My eyes traveled down from Franklin to the iron sconces above the entrance.

Pigeons had taken residence inside.

AIN'T THERE NO LOVE NO MORE?

A FEW DAYS later I got a call from Lyvonne Cargill, Je'Rean's mother. She told me that Je'Rean's best friend, a kid named Chaise Sherrors, had been murdered the night before—an innocent bystander who took a bullet in the head as he was on a porch clipping someone's hair.

"It just goes on," she said. "The silent suffering."

Chaise's mother wanted to talk to someone—anyone—who might think her child was worth something. The job fell to me since I knew there would be no other takers in a city anesthetized to violence.

Chaise lived on the other side of the Chrysler complex. He too was about to graduate from Southeastern High. A good kid who showed neighborhood children how to work electric clippers, his dream was to open a barbershop. The morning after he was shot, Chaise's clippers were mysteriously deposited on his front porch, wiped clean and free of hair. There was no note.

If such a thing could be true, Chaise's neighborhood was worse than Je'Rean's. Walk a mile along Mack Avenue in each direction from Alter Road to Gratiot Avenue. You will count thirty-four churches, a dozen liquor stores, six beauty salons and barbershops, a funeral parlor, a sprawling Chrysler engine and assembly complex working at less than half capacity, and three dollar stores—but no grocery stores. In fact, there are no chain grocery stores in all of Detroit.

The house next door to Chaise's was rubble smelling of burnt pine, pissed all over with spray paint by admirers of the East Warren Crips. The house on the other side was in much the same state. So was the house across the street. In this shit, a one-year-old played next door, barefoot.

Chaise's mother, Britta McNeal, sat on the porch staring blankly into the distance, smoking no-brand cigarettes. She thanked me for coming and showed me her home, which was clean and well kept. Then she introduced me to her fourteen-year-old son, De'Erion, whose remains sat in an urn on the mantel. He was shot in the head and killed the year before, his case unsolved.

She had already cleared a space on the other end of the mantel for Chaise's urn.

"That's a hell of a pair of bookends," I offered.

"You know? I was thinking that," she said with tears.

The daughter of an autoworker and a home nurse, McNeal grew up in the promise of the black middle class that Detroit once offered. But McNeal messed up, she admits as much. She got pregnant at fifteen. She later went to nursing school but got sidetracked by her own health problems. School wasn't a priority. Besides, there was always a job in America when you needed one.

Until there wasn't. Like so many across the country, she's being evicted with no job and no place to go.

"I want to get out of here, but I can't," she said. "I got no money. I'm stuck. Not all of us are blessed."

She looked at her barefoot grandson playing in the wreckage of the dwelling next door and wondered if he would make it to manhood.

"I keep calling about these falling-down houses, but the city never comes," she said.

McNeal wondered how she was going to pay the $3,000 for her son's funeral. Desperation, she said, feels like someone's reaching down your throat and ripping out your guts.

It would be easy to lay the blame on McNeal for the circumstances in which she raised her sons. But is she responsible for police officers with broken computers in their squad cars, firefighters with holes in their boots, ambulances that arrive late, a city that can't keep its lights on and leaves its vacant buildings to the arsonist's match, a state government that allows corpses to stack up in the morgue, multinational corporations that move away and leave poisoned fields behind, judges who let violent criminals walk the streets, school stewards who steal the children's milk money, elected officials who loot the city, automobile executives who couldn't manage a grocery store, or Wall Street grifters who destroyed the economy and left the nation's children with a burden of debt while they partied it up in Southampton?

Can she be blamed for that?

"I know society looks at a person like me and wants me to go away," she said. " 'Go ahead, walk in the Detroit River and disappear.' But I can't. I'm alive. I need help. But when you call for help, it seems like no one's there.

"It feels like there ain't no love no more."

I left McNeal's porch and started my car. The radio was tuned to NPR and *A Prairie Home Companion* came warbling out of my speakers. I stared through the windshield at the little boy in the diaper playing amid the ruins, reached over and switched it off.

PANTS ON FIRE

THE MAN WHO paid the bum twenty bucks to burn down the house that killed firefighter Walt Harris was brought into the courtroom by his elbow.

Mario Willis wore a suit with wide stripes and a jacket hem that hung low on his hips. He sported tasseled loafers and gold-framed glasses and steel handcuffs.

"Who is that, Papa?" my three-year-old daughter squealed.

"He is a man who did bad," I told her. "He's going to jail."

I wasn't a reporter anymore. I was just a stay-at-home dad again, bringing my daughter on a field trip to study the gears of the municipal machinery. I wanted her to see how it was supposed to work, how society looked when it functioned properly. I wanted her to see the good side of things. If the morning's proceedings could be considered good.

And truth be told, I had a pony in this race. I had something to do with this man's punishment. I wanted to feel like I had done at least something for the betterment of Detroit. I wanted to feel . . . happy, I guess.

"What did that bad man do?" my girl asked in her tiny alto.

Even Willis turned around to see where the little voice was coming from.

The bailiff walked over.

"There are no children allowed in the courtroom," she said.

"I'm sorry, I didn't know. She is a citizen," I said hopefully.

The bailiff hesitated, looked around at all the uniformed people who had packed the gallery, and sensing the sadness in the room, she relented. "That's okay, hon. Just try to keep her quiet."

I told my daughter to whisper.

The firehouse mates of Harris sat in the jury box, scowling and whiskered. They looked like one of those old silver daguerreotypes from the Wild West: dark-eyed, mustachioed and the hair miscombed. One of the men looked as though he were preparing to leap out of the box and puncture Willis's throat with a knife.

Willis did not look up at them.

My daughter noticed the dour men in the jurors' box as well.

"Who are they, Papa?"

"Those are firemen."

"Why are they here?"

"They want to see what happens to the bad man."

"What did the bad man do, Papa?" she asked again.

"He killed their friend," I said. "He was my friend too."

"Oh dear," she whispered. "How did your friend die, Papa?"

"By fire."

"Why was he making a fire?"

"He wasn't. The bad man made a fire to burn a house so he could get some money."

"Was it an accident, Pops?"

"No, sweets."

"The bad man, he's still nice. Right, Pops?"

"I don't know, sweetheart," I said, kissing her neck. "That's why we're here. All of us together will decide how nice he is."

"Is your friend in heaven with God?"

"He has to be," I said.

Judge Michael Callahan, a small stone-faced Irishman, entered the courtroom. The people stood.

"Who's he, Papa?"

"He's the judge, sweets. He will decide how long the man will go to jail for killing another man."

"Killing is not right, is it, Pops?"

"No, it is not. God says it is the worst thing a human being can do."

"Yes, Pops. It's very bad."

"And those are lawyers," I pointed out to my daughter. "They will argue how long the man should go to jail."

My daughter quickly grew bored with the lawyers and their arguments and protestations and sentencing guidelines. She ducked beneath the pews to play with her toys on the carpet. I did not stop her.

Willis's mother and then his minister spoke on his behalf—calling his conviction both devastating and unjustified. They spoke about his faith and his work with young toughs. They spoke of the Spirit Award bestowed upon him by the mayor of the city, who was currently residing in the state penitentiary. Their son was a pillar of Detroit, they sobbed. Their son was an honest citizen.

Then came the sickening part. Willis himself. With a straight face, he maintained his innocence despite the fact that the handyman he hired to set the blaze placed him at the scene of the fire. The handyman testified he was paid to burn it down once before. Willis's cell phone records placed him at the scene of the fire. Willis's wife testified that he was sleeping with her that night even though phone records show that Willis called her on his cell phone. His wife testified he must have called her from the next pillow over.

His monologue was so weak, so insulting, so slippery, that some of the jurors who had convicted him at trial and had come for his sentencing hissed like snakes.

"Your Honor," said Willis, standing with an oily but straight face. "I was taught to own up and be a responsible man to all actions. And it's just . . . it's not in me, Your Honor, to own up to anything that I didn't have a part of. I maintain my innocence in this matter."

Most insulting, he turned to the widow of Walt Harris, addressing her directly.

"I apologize to you, Ms. Harris. I hate the loss. You know, I don't like what's happening. I mean because you and your family had the biggest loss ever. I hate that you have been put in this situation, but I did not set this man to do this and I did not have any type of financial gain or any financial wherewithal with this situation. And that's from me to you."

He turned to the ash-faced Callahan. "I just once again, just thank you. I ask you to have mercy upon me and I'm very humbled by the situation."

The widow sobbed at the audacity of the pimp-suited businessman who had cheated her of a beautiful life. Willis the arsonist who burned down a corner of the city for his own profit. Willis the man of God who asked for mercy but could not admit to a widow's face that his greed had cost her husband's life.

He was everything wrong. He took no responsibility for the lives he ruined. He blamed others. He hid behind slogans and excuses. He was Kwame Kilpatrick. He was General Motors. He was Wall Street. He was modern America. He was a cheater.

My daughter, hearing the widow whimper, crawled up on my lap.

The judge's porcelain complexion had gone scarlet as he imposed his sentence:

"In the City of Detroit we have been plagued by arson as a means of entertainment that was known in the city as Devil's Night, a situation in which the firefighters were called on in many instances to battle hundreds of fires," he growled.

"They have also been forced to battle fires in schemes for profit, fires set in order to generate insurance proceeds from those who do not deserve them. The defendant went to great lengths to avoid detection and responsibility in his arson-for-profit scheme, including orchestrating perjury by his wife for use in his alibi defense."

My daughter, who was standing on the pew, whispered in my ear.

"Why is the judge yelling, Papa?"

"The judge is angry because the man is lying," I said.

"He's a liar, Pops?"

"Yes, he's a liar."

"Pants on fire?"

"Yes, Boo Boo. Pants on fire."

Judge Callahan sentenced Willis to forty-two years in prison.

People often ask, where is the hope in Detroit? It was right here. I had just watched it. Society had functioned properly in this case because we all wanted it to. The firefighters, the cops, the judge, the jury, the reporter. We the people who wish to raise our children in peace and health. We the people who would like to bequeath something decent to the people who will follow us. To borrow from George Orwell: People like the cops and the firefighters are willing to commit violence and risk their lives on the behalf of others so others may sleep peacefully at night. People who believed in order and fairness. People clever enough to get away with the lie but who defeat the urge for the greater benefit.

A dirty man had killed our friend. And we got him behind bars. We got justice without harming the law. It felt righteous. In the end, if we are going to fix it, we are going to have to stand up and say "enough" and then get on with the difficult work of cleaning it up.

On my way to the elevator, a group of firefighters including Nevin stopped me.

"Hey, Charlie," he said. "Thank you."

It was only the second time in my journalism career that I remembered someone with an official capacity saying that to me. Thank you. The other time was at Ground Zero when the final piece of debris had been removed from the hole. It was a group of iron workers who until that point acted as though they hated my interloping guts.

"LeDuff. I appreciate you writing our names down," shouted one of them, walking across the bar and handing me a glass of bourbon. "Thank you." I was happy he knew my name. That was enough.

It was the same now.

"You're welcome," I said.

The elevator doors opened.

"Can I push the button, Pops?" my daughter asked.

A woman wearing a blouse tighter than a prophylactic and saucer-sized sunglasses stood in our way.

"Excuse us, please," I said.

She looked like Monica Conyers, the city councilwoman-for-sale who would be sentenced to prison in a few weeks. She said nothing and turned from the doors.

I said nothing and stepped into the elevator.

My daughter pressed the button and we all went down together.

EPILOGUE

KWAME KILPATRICK WASN'T the first Detroit politician to milk the city. It had been going on for a hundred years. And it wasn't just the politicians. It was union bosses and contractors and industrialists and receptionists who were nieces of the connected. Everybody got their piece and that was all right when Detroit was rolling in money. There were always enough paychecks to paper over the maggots.

But now there isn't. At the time of this printing Detroit finds itself in the midst of a bankruptcy and under the control of an unelected emergency manager. It is the largest Chapter 9 filing in U.S. history. With no ability to borrow, the Motor City is unable to pay its pension obligations or honor its health care promises to its retirees and current employees.

In order to make basic payroll in Detroit, ambulances are allowed to break down, hydraulic fire trucks are grounded because they have never been inspected, and police have no working radios when they enter buildings.

In the meantime, places like Los Angeles are in the same predicament, ten-fold. Like I said: Detroit was the first up, first down, but never alone.

Kilpatrick was convicted on twenty-four counts ranging from extortion to racketeering to bribery. He ran a mob-style enterprise that stole from the poorest people in America and then tried to play it off with the old Eight Mile race card—even though some of his biggest backers were the rich white industrialists who profited from the confusion. A neat piece of theater that got bad reviews.

He was sentenced to twenty-eight years in prison, the longest sentence for public corruption in the history of the country.

Monica Conyers was sent to Camp Cupcake, a minimum-security federal prison in West Virginia, for a three-year bid. The time there is easy. Martha Stewart served five months for lying to the FBI and managed to lose some weight. There is no razor wire and inmates get a hair dryer. Still, it wasn't good enough for Madam Conyers. She complained in letters to the press that they wouldn't give her seconds at supper. She said she was bored. She asked the federal judge to let her serve the remainder of her sentence at home on Seven Mile Road with her son, who never bothered to mow the lawn. Her request was denied. She was eventually paroled and worked for a time at an automobile repair shop.

Chief Evans and his career might have survived the accidental shooting of the little girl. He had brought murder way down during his year as the top cop. And he really had brought it down. Not by lying about the number of bodies and hiding them behind excuses, like his predecessors, but by turning the police loose and holding them accountable. Citizens were complaining that the police were too tough, but at least they were alive to complain.

Chief Evans might have survived the shooting of the little girl had he too not been drawn to the lights of Hollywood. As it turns out, Evans was filming a pilot for his own reality show entitled "The Chief."

The six-minute sizzle-reel begins with Evans dressed in full battle gear in front of the shattered Michigan Central Rail Depot cradling a semiautomatic rifle and declaring that he would "do whatever it takes" to take back the streets of Detroit. Evans was fired.

But in Evans's defense, he seemed to understand one thing: after the collapse of the car industry and the implosion of the real estate bubble, there is little else Detroit has to export except its misery.

Lt. Mike Nevin got his job back, winning yet another lawsuit against the city. He continues to jump into burning buildings. Fire Commissioner James Mack and his deputies were fired after I reported that they were engaged in a cover-up of the theft of a citizen's property by a firefighter. A new man was brought in from Los Angeles. The stealing apparently stopped, but nothing else improved.

In the meantime, Detroit continues to struggle. A quarter million people fled the city in the first decade of the twenty-first century, bringing its population to less than 700,000—a hundred-year low.

Evans's successor, Chief Ralph Godbee, took a kinder, gentler approach to policing. Predictably, murder spiraled out of control, reaching levels not seen in a generation, taking the population decline into account. The fudging of the crime statistics began anew. And Godbee, who moonlighted as a preacher, would abruptly retire when it was revealed that he had bedded a bevy of female officers.

General Motors and Chrysler continue to make cars thanks in large part to the American taxpayer, who bailed them out (and are still owed billions of dollars), and their creditors, who took it in the shorts and received almost nothing for their investment. Ford too is profitable again. But for the first time ever, more cars were sold in China than in the United States.

American Axle moved much of the remainder of its Detroit jobs out of state and country. The stock moved up. The factory buildings in Detroit are scheduled to be torn down.

Detroit, I am sure, will continue to be. Just as Rome does. What it will be and who will be here, I cannot say. We have profitable car companies. At least $150 billion in trade with Canada crossing over Matty Moroun's bridge. Reinvestment downtown. The Feds helping us with our political corruption and our municipal balance sheet.

But the unnecessary and unskilled human beings will have to find some other place to go and something else to do. The Great Remigration south, maybe. At least you don't have heating bills down there.

Sadly, Sgt. Mike Martel, the homicide detective, died after he lost control of his motorcycle and struck a telephone pole. His very big heart was donated to a stranger. My cousin Johnny died in a bike wreck too. I don't know what became of his organs.

My brother Frankie got a new place to live and a new used car to drive. He teaches college. My brother Bill was selling motivational speaking engagements for a prominent motivational speaker until nobody had the motivation to listen anymore. He's working for the Yellow Pages now. My brother Jim plugs along. My mother is a widow now that her husband, my stepdad, Warren, passed away. We'll all be okay. They raise them strong on Joy Road.

There was still one place I had left to go: the Brightmoor section of the city. The site of my sister's death. I needed to go back to the bar where my mother sat so elegantly in her raccoon coat among the filth, sipping Jack Daniel's, trying to find some explanation for my sister's ruined life and, receiving none, going home brokenhearted.

Since my return to Detroit, I have seen my sister everywhere: every time I saw a rough-looking white woman with a limp, in every old woman locked in her house. I had avoided the neighborhood for a decade, but I had to confront that ghost. My sister counted, and the living people count too. We're still here and we're always going to be. I was in need of an answer when I didn't even know the question.

The Flame Bar was located around Five Mile and Telegraph, on the far west side of the city. It is a big intersection, but it was a hard place to find—the city had fallen into such disrepair that it looked like it had been dropped from the third-floor window by its hair. I drove past the shattered storefronts, then the roaming dogs, then the churches that didn't seem to make any difference, then the leathery prostitutes and then a giant cinder-block bar painted pink, the doors wide open, the parking lot full. There was no sign.

I pulled in. There was soul music spilling into the street. The Reverend Al Green. The place was pretty in its way, as much as it could be, like a daisy in a field full of rust.

I approached a group of black men having a cigarette around a Ford Econoline. One lowered his bottle wrapped in a paper bag like I was a cop.

"I'm looking for the Flame Bar," I said. "I remember it was around here somewhere."

"This used to be the Flame Bar," said one of the men, Tyrone. "What you need?"

"I don't know," I said, and explained my mind and my sister.

The suspicious man softened. He handed me his bottle.

"This bar changed six years ago," Tyrone said. "They trying to put something nice up in this shit hole. Can't say it's working. But what you gonna do? You ain't gonna be reincarnated, so you got to do the best you can with the moment you got. Do the best you can and try to be good. You dig?"

I did. We are born to a time. What you do with it is on you. Do the best you can. Try to be good. And live.

I went into the bar. It was a clean, dimly lit place with a pool table with a bulb over it and some photographs of old soul singers taped to the mirror. People were laughing. There were doors on the toilet thresholds, another improvement since the last time I'd been here. Tyrone bought me a drink.

The sun was setting low through the open door. Despite the good feelings, I remembered what the prostitute near the mosque told me: I don't work past sunset. They crazy motherfuckers out here.

I bought a round and left. Then I drove northerly, up a side street, looking for the vacant lot where my sister died. After having the last drink of her life, my sister rode away with a strange man. It must have been a scene of insanity and adrenaline and purple haze. She jumped out the door. And into a tree.

I found the lot. I parked the car and didn't lock it. I didn't think I needed to. The block was utterly abandoned, the shells of homes where middle-class lives were once lived. The same homes were occupied the last time I was here with my mother. The collapse came on and it came on quickly. Like a tsunami. I don't know if it was drugs that ruined the neighborhood or civic neglect. Was it the disappearance of the car jobs or the raping of the middle class by Wall Street? Had people just given up? I didn't know. But it hurt to look at it. Vanity. In the end, it was all vanity.

The grass in the field was neck-high, so high in fact I couldn't make out the tree. The mosquitoes were greedy. I stood in the field thinking of my sister and that picture of her on the junior high basketball team, dressed in knee-high socks and a green tank top with LOWELL LANCERS lettered across the chest, dribbling a ball, smiling. I thought of my own daughter, who looks like my sister in a way. I thought about my ancestors and all they had done to deliver me here to this spot. I thought of all that and cried a little bit through my cigarette.

Then the grass rustled, startling me. Someone or something was coming on, but I couldn't see through the tall stalks. I began to panic, realizing I was left high in the weeds, no knife, no gun, only a pen.

They crazy motherfuckers out here.

That's when she stopped in front of me, not ten feet away, unafraid. A spotted fawn, a pretty little thing, barely thigh-high, with black bulbous eyes that didn't seem to fit her skull.

In that field of death covered with vines and grass, it was true what Tyrone said. You ain't gonna be reincarnated, so do the best with the moment you got.

I don't believe in reincarnation either, but I do believe in symbolism.

"Hey girl," I whispered to the fawn, "where's your mama?"

The beast sniffed once, turned away and off she ran into the wild city.

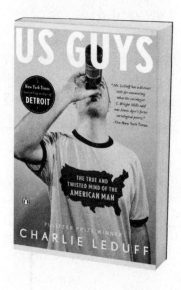